TALES FROM THE TRAIL

STORIES FROM THE OLDEST HIKER HOSTEL
ON THE APPALACHIAN TRAIL

SHERRY BLACKMAN

Published by Mindstir Media, LLC
45 Lafayette Rd | Suite 181| North Hampton, NH 03862 | USA
1.800.767.0531 | www.mindstirmedia.com

MINDSTIR MEDIA

Printed in the United States of America
ISBN-13: 978-1-7376287-3-6

May your trails be crooked, winding, lonesome, dangerous, leading to the most amazing view. May your mountains rise into and above the clouds.

Edward Abbey, American writer (1927-1989)

I dedicate this book to the generations of the Presbyterian Church of the Mountain who worked tirelessly to provide hospitality to hikers from around the world and to the generations who will continue the ministry into the future.

I dedicate this collection to all hikers—past, present, and future—who shared their stories of struggles and brokenness, and found healing, mercy, and compassion in the cathedral of the wild.

In particular, I dedicate this book to David Childs, wilderness guide, teacher, and leader, who faithfully served the Hiker Ministry day and night for more years than any of us can count.

TABLE OF CONTENTS

PREFACE

D URING THE 2020 PANDEMIC, ONE THING held true: Scores of
people headed out for a day hike on the Appalachian Trail (AT)
as if being in the woods, immersed in beauty and mystery, immunized
them against an invisible enemy. The AT became a hospital for souls
locked up in quarantine, needing to breathe, stretch, and be nourished
by the earth beneath their feet.

For decades, the AT has been a sanctuary for seekers, the tired and
the lost; those hungry for renewal, the broken and the grieving; and
those who want to face and answer questions they have lugged around
with them in invisible backpacks. Questions like, what is next for me?
Is there a God? Should I live or end it all? How can I liberate my life
from what weighs it down? How can I forgive God?

This book pays tribute to those who dare such a grueling and soul-
satisfying adventure. It tells the tales of those on a pilgrimage through
insightful conversations and encounters, exploring and revealing what
angels the hikers wrestle with in the wilderness who call out to name
them again. This collection unveils the spirituality of any such journey
in sometimes humorous, sometimes heart-wrenching portraits.

Tales from the Trail explores what it means to be human.

IN THE BLEAK MIDWINTER

The heart's awakening is the true work of our lives.

Mary Oliver

I FORCE THE KEY INTO THE cold hard lock of the Hikers Center and shoulder the door open. The freezing wind rushes in as I shut the door fast behind me, then push open the old, narrow french doors to the common area. Inside the one-windowed room, there is nothing but winter darkness. Only a heavy curtain is drawn to keep out the chill. I press in the century's old light switch. The sign-in sheets are blank, waiting for inscription. Everything is neat and tidy now with the absence of hikers over the last couple of weeks, but a few are on their way, having already started in Georgia and will arrive in March or April. Yet, it's as if the air itself is imprinted with all those who have stayed here. The room is crowded with them. I sense them, their sweat-soaked, over-worn clothes, the animal smells their bodies emit as if all hikers are in heat, both male and female pheromones mix with the air's undercurrents.

I'm grateful for this break, although a part of me misses the daily adventure of heading up the church driveway and seeing all kinds of people hanging about, their gear and clothes hung out or spread on the asphalt to dry. I sink into the human silence of the room. The furnace kicks on with an occasional clank. I'm grateful for the warmth. Regretfully, the door has to be locked to prevent the homeless from bunking down inside the center this time of year. For this moment, no one will know to come to find me here; I can be quiet, undisturbed, and process the season of hospitality that has passed. There were so many hikers with whom I had no opportunity to engage in any meaningful conversation, mostly because there were too many people around. Vulnerability requires honor and protection, and everyone is vulnerable. I've gained a certain kind of courage by listening to hikers, both young and old, who have pushed forward, despite bruises and blisters, muscles that never stop burning, insect bites, rashes, and shin splints. They persevered when they wanted nothing more than to give up, going beyond what they thought were their limits, steered by that inner drive to accomplish what they set out to do, no matter what.

On the coffee table in front of me is the year's journal that I flip through. Each page of paper feels like skin between my fingers. Many left notes to fellow hikers who will hunker down here for a night or two, advising them where to go in town, where the best meals were, or they shared some epiphany in words or drawings.

For some reason, Trillium comes to mind. She was the first hiker who introduced herself to me, the newly-called minister, on my initial Sunday here at Church of the Mountain, June 1, 2014. Trillium had graduated college in December and set out on the AT alone from Georgia in February. She had long, soft blonde hair and green eyes, and she tilted her head slightly to the right when she listened.

After worship, she waited to talk with me until I had greeted everyone from the congregation. She said she hadn't been in church since she was a young teen. She told me that she was deeply moved by the service and couldn't wait to call her parents and tell them she had attended church. She did not know it, but she spoke "forest" to me that morning—there was fertility to her words that grew me as if each word was a seed. Maybe it was just that sense of her being so present, so affirming, on my first day.

Later that afternoon, she and I sat at the picnic table outside the center, and we spoke about her experience hiking the trail as a single woman. She taught me how hikers adopt trail names usually given by another hiker or hikers, although she said she chose her own. I thought the anonymity of such names freed hikers from being who they were in the world they left behind. She decided on the name Trillium, a single three-petaled wildflower that shoots out from a whorl of three leaves and grows among other trilliums, off by themselves, hiding from others, hidden from full view, blooming alone. She said it was her favorite flower growing up.

I marveled at her fearlessness. She shared that she felt safer on the AT than she ever felt in the civilized world. Her eyes looked as if they had bits of mica in them, shimmering in the afternoon light. We talked of the spiritual aspect of her journey, of the magnetic pull of nature itself toward the Source of all things. She thanked me for our conversation, said she needed to talk about such things, and didn't know it. We shared the language of roots—speaking of invisible things that hold everything together.

What happened after she reached Mount Katahdin? Chances are, I would never know; I doubt she'd ever find her way back here again. If she did, I would ask her if the experience of being on the trail was always present for her. Did her love for the natural world deepen every day into an ache that called her incessantly to feel the earth's pulse beneath her feet, bidding her to lay flat on the ground and feel the spine of roots beneath her own? Or, like many love affairs, would it be a longing for what had passed, with no way to ever get back to that moment, to that place, to those arms, despite the gravitational pull?

Maybe it was because she was the first hiker I had engaged with, but I knew I would never stop wondering about her. I don't remember where she was from or what her ambitions were once she finished the trail.

I close the journal and stand up. All is well here. The room itself holds its breath, waiting for the next sojourner to enter, fall into its arms, wash in its stream, and feel the warmth of this underground cave. It's cradling me, insisting that I understand that when I behold another, their voice becomes part of my own, their touch becomes part of my skin, their breath a part of my lungs.

ROCKS OF AGES

Humans of dust, we are nothing but a story.

St. Columba

EXCERPT FROM HIKERS CENTER JOURNAL, DATED JULY 24, 1998:

I had a dream that I stood before God. He said to me, "You are one of the chosen. You may enter heaven for eternal life."

"If it's all the same to you," I said, "When my time comes, just snuff me out. I don't want to live for an eternity."

"Little one, what do you know of eternity?" He asked.

"Oh, I know all about it," I said. "I've walked over the rocks of PA."

JOURNALIST DON HOPEY, WRITING FOR the *Cape Cod Times*, July 30, 1995, started to name the rocks of Pennsylvania: "Rocky Raccoon, Rocket Man, Rock Lobster, Crocodile Rock, Rock and Rye, Roxanne," he wrote. "Thru-hikers know it as 'ninety miles of hell.'"

In the same article, hiker Beorn (trail name) is quoted as saying that the rocks are in conversation with each other, teaming up to stop hikers. "There are vampire rocks—they want your blood," he said.

"There are hip rocks that just want a little skin. And some rocks can jump. They grab your boot just when you think you've got it clear."

Up the road a few miles from the church, bordering on Kirkridge Retreat Center on the slopes of Blue Mountain, resides a man with rocks in his heart. Ancient, monumental ones, I should say. He has rocks in his head, too. At least that's what started his vision for what is now Columcille Megalith Park, fashioned after Isle of Iona (located on the Inner Hebrides off the western coast of Scotland). He calls it a place for "reluctant saints and weary sinners." The Reverend William Cohea, Jr., more of a self-proclaimed druid than Presbyterian minister, wanted his own mystical isle in the Appalachian Mountains of Pennsylvania. I came to talk to him about his two-year stint at the Church of the Mountain, beginning in 1976, when the Hikers Ministry was established.

Leaning upon a walking stick that was gnarled and crooked and as bent as his body, Rev. Cohea met me outside his home that stands guard over Columcille. He wore his signature blue captain's hat that shaded his sun-marked face, a pale yellow cotton jacket, and gray sweatpants that sagged over his frail ninety-year-old body. In his left hand was a pipe that he lifted to his mouth and clenched between his stained teeth, drawing out the impossible last puff of smoke. He had a sonorous, baritone voice as if he was preaching even while in quiet conversation, with a little raspiness lacing what seemed like rationed breath and word. On a hot and humid day, his breaths were shallow and frequent as he shuffled toward his house, planting the end of his walking stick into the dry earth in front of him and pulling himself forward. Since he was a little shaky and unsteady, I reached out and clutched his arm. He shook off my hand like a pesky insect.

"I'm just fine, honey," he said. "Here we are, Casa Colum."

Entering his domicile, the scent of cherry pipe tobacco hung pleasantly in the air, mixed with the fragrance of old wood fires emitting from two stone fireplaces in the large living room. His elderly border collie greeted us, panting and eyeballing us through cloudy blue eyes. Some of the furniture looked plucked from a church or an old cathedral—throne-like oak chairs with red velvet cushions, a short pew, and a long thick wooden slab of a table topped with large and heavy books. Their rotting leather covers left brownish dust near their spines. Everywhere I looked, there were too many chairs—threadbare overstuffed chairs and wooden chairs that I had to wend my way around.

The house was full of primeval energy; it seemed crowded with unseen ancestors. This place where I had never visited before felt like coming home in a way I couldn't explain.

We walked through the room toward the screened-in porch that gave an unobstructed view of the pond with orange and white koi and a few large standing stones alongside its edge. On the other side of the porch was Cohea's office that overflowed with books, papers, files, tickets, souvenirs, and a bed.

We settled into rocking chairs on the porch. A hot breeze blew over us, offering no relief from the July heat. He tamped some tobacco into his pipe and lit it, then rocked back and forth, talking as he did about Columcille—how it came to be, how he had rocks brought in from faraway places, how he and his late partner had a vision decades ago that was now a reality. The porch was his throne room, and he, as king, could overlook his kingdom.

He spoke at length about his deceased life partner of several decades, his ex-wife, his four children, one son who had died in middle age of a heart attack, and of a grandchild who had been killed in a car accident two years ago.

"Life happens," he said, pausing, it seemed to me, to let sorrow flow through him. "I've outlived seven cardiologists. Let's go for a tour, shall we?"

I agreed with a bit of apprehension. "Are we going to walk?"

"No, we'll take the golf cart."

We headed out the front door; Cohea flopped himself onto the hard plastic seat of the cart and flipped on the key. Off we went, careening up and down steep knolls. I held my breath, whispering one inaudible prayer after another, sure we were going to tumble over with every accelerated ascent and uncontrolled descent. We drove by rocks that were intentionally placed in a Stonehenge design. Other stones appeared as randomly placed sculptures, organically shaped like little cathedrals with no doors. Cohea knew each one by name as if they were living creatures. I believe to him they were—primordial unmovable guards, allowing entrance only to those who were willing to press ear and knee to earth and be still.

We stopped abruptly in front of St. Columba's Chapel, a small circular stone building. Inside, it was cool and damp, a refuge from the heat. It felt like an in-between place, thin-space, where the invisible is more palpable than the visible. He showed me the moveable stones laid into the floor. Beneath one were placed his partner's ashes; he stood on the stone next to it where his ashes would go when the time came.

As the golf cart droned on, Cohea spoke about the Hikers Ministry and about what the Church of the Mountain was like forty-five years ago. In the 70s, the congregation's "faithful fifteen," as they were often referred to, rejected gay ministers, and so Cohea's time there was short-lived.

When speaking of faith, he said, "It's not theology, it's *weology*. It's about the oneness of all."

What I heard was: "I've rejected the rejection and insisted on being acceptable to God. It's about us, not Him."

"Doctrine is nonsense," he continued. "Dogma is bullshit; hospitality is everything."

He had graduated from Princeton Seminary in 1952 and was ordained the same year. Being a man of faith and religious conscience, he had to find a way for both holy and human acceptance in an era when the two seemed incompatible.

"The Hikers Ministry was about hospitality, not dogma."

In other words, the church was to embrace the stranger with the pure and straightforward agenda of caring for hikers without forcing the gospel upon them. The congregation's hands and feet were to be the only sermon preached.

What he said about sermons being spoken through service was still true. But, there were always words—words of welcome, of engagement, of kindness. At Thursday night potluck dinners during the summer, hikers shared an abundance of gratitude, and those who served carved out large spaces for listening. Words have always been and will always be essential. Cohea knew that. What he meant, I was sure, was to use them as bread and wine are used for communion—as nourishment of the inward life, for stirring the appetite for spiritual things, and as an invitation to discern what is meaningful and what is life-giving.

"In 1976, we surveyed the hikers, what their needs were, how many came through Delaware Water Gap. We consulted with the Appalachian Trail Conservancy. Back then, hikers would get their resupply boxes from the post office right next to the church, and you would see them unpacking and repacking their packs, spreading their goods out wherever they could find a patch of green grass on the lower churchyard. In all, that first year, we counted about three hundred hikers passing through," he said.

People from the congregation started to invite hikers home, offering them a shower and doing their laundry. Over time, the basement of the sanctuary was transformed into a shelter; at first, there were cots, then bunks were built, and a bathroom and shower were later installed.

Cohea stopped the cart a short distance from Thor's Gate, a five-stone structure, two upright stones per side, and one across the top, marking the entrance to one of the trails that looped through the surrounding woods. He engaged with a few visitors who were walking the grounds. The largeness of his laughter drew me in as it did the others. It was clear to me, and anyone who spoke with him, that Columcille was his legacy, a place of wonder, silence, contemplation, and perhaps more than anything else, mysticism. It would remain long after he was gone, continuing to be a place to walk, meditate, stare into stones, rocks and sun-filtered forests, and watch for that veil between worlds to burn away and reveal all things.

I invited him to come to the church that upcoming Sunday to speak during the celebration of the Hikers Ministry's 40th anniversary. Before I left him at Casa Colum, he gave me two booklets that he had authored, *From the Beginning to the Beginning* and *Come Dance with Me*. Both covers had a photograph of him wearing his captain's hat, pipe in mouth and hand, with Columcille in the background. Inside the booklet *Come Dance with Me*, he scribbled in pen the words "Christ the active verb of the mysterious what is."

"Perhaps we are to work out our salvation with diligence—to have a love affair with mystery and to respect the unknown that surrounds us," I read as I flipped through the pages.

A quote from Thomas Merton stood out like one of the stones of Columcille:

> *The rush and pressure of modern life are a form, perhaps the most common form, of its innate violence. To allow oneself to be carried away by a multitude of conflicting concerns, to surrender to too many demands, to commit oneself to too many people and projects, to want to help everyone in everything is to succumb to violence.*[1]

The following Sunday, when Cohea stepped up to the pulpit, his voice bellowed and fell to almost a whisper. His presence and theatrics demanded attention. He congratulated the congregation for forty years of a job well done, for the diligence the Hikers Ministry required.

"I was there in the beginning," he said as if he was as old as Genesis. Then he lifted the large Bible slightly off the pulpit and said, "This is nonsense. It's about *weology*."

I squirmed.

"This church has a legacy of hospitality that goes beyond dogma and doctrine." What was supposed to be a five-minute sermon lengthened into twenty minutes.

Afterward, along with several hikers, the congregation joined in the celebratory brunch, followed by cake and ice cream. Only a few of the "faithful fifteen" were still alive to tell the stories of how the ministry started, how it had grown over the decades, and how it became a cornerstone of the church.

---

1   Merton, Thomas. Conjectures of a Guilty Bystander (Reissue Edition, 1968) 81

DELAWARE WATER GAP

(A LITTLE HISTORY)

A few minutes ago every tree was excited, bowing to the roaring storm, waving, swirling, tossing their branches in glorious enthusiasm like worship. But though to the outer ear these trees are now silent, their songs never cease. Every hidden cell is throbbing with music and life, every fibre thrilling like harp strings, while incense is ever flowing from the balsam bells and leaves. No wonder the hills and groves were God's first temples, and the more they are cut down and hewn into cathedrals and churches, the farther off and dimmer seems the Lord.

John Muir

THE DELAWARE WATER GAP NATIONAL Recreation Area encompasses seventy thousand acres, located midway along the Delaware River in New Jersey and Pennsylvania. When driving on Route 80, either westbound or eastbound through the Gap, I am in awe of the looming mountains, sharp-toothed cliffs, and the ravine between them where the river flows. Wherever you look after a rainfall or melting snow, waterfalls cascade over shale and slate. Here is a story of glaciers and ancient stones, Native Americans, and the missionaries that came to convert them. The Delaware Water Gap was the second most visited resort area in the country during the 1800s and early 1900s for

New York City and Philadelphia residents. Many of the river resort houses are gone, their charred ruins buried in the mountainsides.

Today, about four million people visit the park annually from all over the world. During the pandemic, longing to be in the great outdoors and inhale the wood-scented air, thousands of visitors came every day. The numbers are not yet in for 2020. Most come not only for the spectacular scenery but also for the Appalachian Trail for a day hike. The 2,200-mile Trail starts at Springer Mountain, Georgia, ends at Mount Katahdin, Maine, and runs through the Delaware Water Gap National Recreation Area. On the map, the trail is drawn in red, perhaps as a way to speak for the sheer strength and determination required to walk it, for the blood that will be shed along the way, for blisters endured, and for blackened toenails lost. The trail wounds those who walk it with its demands and beauty, its wildness and solitude. It challenges hikers to know themselves as they have never known themselves before.

The town of Delaware Water Gap lies within the narrow gorge at the river's bend. In 2014, it was officially named an Appalachian Trail Town. It's home to the Deer Head Inn, one of the oldest, continuously-running jazz clubs in the country. Across the street is the Castle Inn, the last remaining resort, where Fred Waring (known for the Waring Blender and big band music) established the Shawnee Press, a music publication. Next door to the Deer Head Inn is the Presbyterian Church of the Mountain, which houses the oldest, continuously-running thru-hiker hostel on the AT.

Up the church's steep driveway, one sees tents pitched on the grassy knoll along the edge of the parking lot, plastic chairs doubling as clotheslines with underwear, pants, shorts, soiled and stiff socks drying in the sun and wind. Packs are airing out. Hiking boots, creased and worn with miles, with soles sliced from Pennsylvania's sharp rocks, lean against the old red brick sanctuary, next to dented and muddy trekking poles.

The Hikers Center was established in the stained-glass sanctuary's basement in 1976, one hundred and twenty-three years after the church was built. A bell tower rings on the hour throughout the day, and at noon and six in the evening, songs play from the carillon. This tradition in the past told travelers where sanctuary may be sought and found; today, it guides hikers to the center.

The church's history harkens back to David and John Brainerd, who were missionaries to the Lenape Indians when it was originally called Mountain Church, its cornerstone dated 1852. At the dedication, Rev. F.F. Ellinwood said this:

> *For many centuries past has Jehovah dwelt in the rocky fastness of this mountain. Ere there was a human ear to listen, His voice was uttered here in the sighing of the breeze and the thunder of the storms, which even then were wont to writhe in the close grapple of this narrow gorge. Ere one human footstep had invaded the wildness of the place, or the hand of art had applied the drill and blast to the silent rock, God's hand was working here alone—delving out its deep, rugged pathway, for yonder river and clothing those gigantic bluffs and terraces with undying verdure, and the far gleaming brightness of their laurel bloom. Every day since that first dawn whereat the morning stars sang joyfully together, has God been present here, in Nature's broad temple, which is alone adequate to the indwelling of the infinite one; but never, until this day, has He dwelt there in a temple made with hands.*

Rev. Horatio S. Howell pastored here until he joined the 19th Pennsylvanian Regiment as a chaplain during the Civil War. On July 1, 1863, he was ministering to wounded soldiers during the Battle of Gettysburg in front of the crowded Gettysburg Hospital (housed in the Presbyterian Church in Gettysburg). A group of charging "rebels" deliberately fired their weapons at all who might be in the streets or on the hospital's steps. There is a historical marker at the base of the stairs where Rev. Howell fell to his death.

I doubt that either reverend could have imagined any part of this consecrated space being dedicated to trail-weary sojourners, even though they believed every one of us is a traveler and a wanderer in this life. Or that the Great Indian Warpath that traversed these mountains—also once used for trade and commerce—would become a foot-path where the most daunting war fought was the one people carried around within themselves.

Time is what hikers trade for a walk in the woods, often forfeiting all that they own, withdrawing from loved ones and friends, in search of a way to belong to no one but themselves or to find the One to whom all things belong. They wake up every morning inside a cathedral of trees, where every branch is a steeple, pointing in all directions, for there is nowhere where God is not.

Called to serve as pastor here in 2014, this ministry to wanderers is what drew me. I wanted to belong to a church that engaged in this kind of hospitality, without any overt evangelistic agenda; a church that focused both outward and inward. It seemed to me that the congregation was living out the gospel in a way that I had not seen before.

Thru-hikers, both northbound (NOBO) and southbound (SOBO), come from all over the world and stay a night or two. Here are stories of hikers who have stayed at the center (about fourteen hundred hikers on average each year): Stories of old men grieving the loss of loved ones, young men delaying the responsibilities of adulthood, wounded warriors walking off traumatic stress, broken men and women seeking wholeness, a couple wed on the trail, and a personal story about baptizing my grandson in one of the streams that rush alongside the trail.

On the AT, there is an order and rhythm to the seasons and days. Hikers reflect on the larger miracles in nature's smaller miracles, the shape of the divine hand in every leaf. The wind whispers and calls out, promises hikers they are never alone, insists they lay down their burdens. Only carry the wilderness inside them, the trail says, wherever they go, for everything that happens here has to do with everything else.

NEVER QUIT

One of the lessons learned during the Vietnam War was that the depiction of wounded soldiers, of coffins stacked higher than their living guards, had a negative effect on the viewing public. The military in Iraq specifically banned the photographing of wounded soldiers and coffins, thus sanitizing this terrible and bloody conflict.

Walter Dean Myers

"MA'AM, MY NAME IS JASON, and I'm at the Hikers Center. I'm calling to tell you that I'm here with my truck, helping my buddy on the trail," said the polite male voice on the other end of the phone.

"Well," I said, "we don't usually allow car support for hikers. Our center is for thru-hikers only."

"I'm in a wheelchair, ma'am. I have no legs."

"Oh, oh, well, let me call you back. Can I call you on this number?"

"Yes, ma'am."

I phoned David Childs, who comes daily to help at the center. "David, we have a man at the center who is in a wheelchair and has no legs. He's giving car support to a hiker friend. I am not going to hell for this—you can go to hell for this, but I'm not."

He laughed and agreed that we could make an exception. I called Jason back.

"Jason, you're welcome to stay. I'm not sure how easy it will be to get into the center with a wheelchair."

"I'll manage just fine, ma'am. Thank you."

Later that evening, I found Jason sitting in a wheelchair outside my office, his truck alongside, with a motorized dune-buggy-type ATV in the truck bed. He was waiting for his buddy to meet him here.

I imagined that Jason once stood at about six feet tall—he was muscular, tattooed, clean-cut, a double amputee with stumps just below his groin. He had reddish-brown hair, dark eyes, and a trim beard.

"I lost my legs in Iraq, ma'am, from a roadside bomb while serving with the United States Marine Corps. I can't wear prosthetics—there isn't enough bone left to attach them." He lifted each stump with his right hand to show me, his pant legs folded and pinned over each one. From the way he released each one, they appeared soft and fleshy. "Lost 'em on my ninth and final deployment. Me and my buddy, the hiker, were on the frontline team that surveilled for roadside bombs."

Tattooed on the underside of his right forearm were the words "NEVER QUIT."

"We learned that in the Marines, ma'am. Never quit, no matter what. I never quit. I climbed Mount Katahdin on my stumps, pulling myself up by holding onto a rope. I don't let not having any legs stop me from much. Couldn't hike the trail, though, so I'm offering vehicle support."

I felt a mixture of gratitude and awe in his presence, as well as pity that he didn't want—he saw it in my eyes, the same way I saw a toughness in his. It was as if he repelled all sympathy as if sympathy itself was a symptom of weakness. He had accomplished much since his injury—he would never quit being, doing, living.

"It took me two years of trying to walk—tried every prosthetic out there, but couldn't do it. I get along pretty well without any. I took a shower in the center."

"How were you able to maneuver in there?" The stall was narrow and around a sharp corner.

"I managed with my arms. I took some towels, placed them on the floor, and one on the bottom of the shower stall, and I was able to shower."

How does a man who has so much pride in his duty, carrying the weight of the United States Marine Corps on his shoulders, lose his legs and maintain his sense of dignity?

Jason's hiking buddy arrived around seven that night, along with a female companion. If I were to give the man a trail name upon first sight, I would have named him Scarecrow, for he was tall and lean, with wiry blond hair sticking out everywhere. He walked slightly bent, not unlike other hikers when they release the weight of their pack. Scarecrow had worn only a small, light daypack since Jason was providing support.

"I'm not going to sleep inside the center," he told Jason. "I can't be around a crowd of people." His voice was shaky and hoarse as if slightly unhinged from his vocal cords.

Inside the center were about eight hikers that night and a half dozen camping on the grounds. Scarecrow wasn't a young man, but he wasn't an older man either. His skin was a grayish hue as if all his blood was coursing only to his most vital organs. His eyes were on high alert—super vigilant, roaming corners, surveilling people and places.

I learned that Scarecrow had suffered such a blow to his spine that his nerves were ripped from his spinal cord. He was alive by a small machine attached to the base of his spine that sent electrical pulses through his detached nerves to his heart and lungs. He could never go at a pace that required any acceleration. Learning that, I hated myself for naming him Scarecrow. I would have named him Hero instead.

How many times had those moments of trauma replayed themselves in both Jason's and Hero's memories, if they had any recall at all? With each replay, was there a re-injuring? When did the memory become just a chapter of their life rather than the entire story? These two, it seemed to me, insisted on pursuing adventures and achieving things that even *whole* men and women didn't dare do. In so doing, they proved to the world that sent them to war that they were complete human beings, whether they had legs or not, or whether they had an attached nervous system or not. What made them whole was the same thing that makes anyone whole—love and a soul to hold it and give it.

They were warriors even now in full combat, with enemies whose names were depression, despair, suicide, and anxiety. I witnessed in these two men that their bodies were blown apart, but the illusion of being safe in the world was shattered forever. I had seen that before with other veterans on the trail but none as injured as these two.

After being on active duty in some of the harshest places on earth, American life seemed superficial to returning troops, they told me. People were unwilling to sacrifice the smallest of conveniences and were too lazy, entitled, distracted, and apathetic. I do not know, but I imagine that gunfire and roadside bombs and hand grenades breech a spiritual sound barrier with each sonic boom that thunders around them.

Jason stayed behind the next morning while Hero hiked out to finish a section of the trail, so he took other hikers into town to resupply. He shared his stories with them—not of war, but of what he had done since that day he'd learned he would have to walk with his arms and hands. How he'd climbed mountains, pitched the first ball at a major league baseball game, and met the President of the United States.

The following day, Jason packed his truck with his friend's gear and headed toward the next rendezvous point where he'd meet up with Hero. They were there for each other in life as they had been there for each other in near death.

As I watched Jason drive away, I kept asking myself, would the rest of us be there for them.

LONGINGS

Spirituality is not to be learned by flight from the world,
or by running away from things, or by turning solitary
and going apart from the world. Rather, we must learn an
inner solitude wherever or with whomsoever we may be.
We must learn to penetrate things and find God there.

Meister Eckhart

ISO—SHORT FOR IN SEARCH OF—WAS an American expatriate living somewhere in the Pacific for ten years before hiking the trail in 2015. He sent me an email two years after he had thru-hiked the AT and stayed at the church. He would be section-hiking mid-August and asked if we could meet when he arrived in Delaware Water Gap, where he would eventually join two friends. He would stay next door at the Deer Head Inn before heading out to hike and wanted to meet on a Wednesday evening after I was finished at a local truck stop where I serve as a chaplain.

I looked forward to hearing about what had transpired in his life. Did he find healing while hiking the AT, did his appetite for life return? Last I had seen him, he was so thin, wore a jagged beard, and his hair long. He carried sorrow back then. His wife of seven years, a highly respected professional, had an affair, and he was hiking to place some distance between them in an attempt to forgive her and let her go. He had abandoned a high-paying career to do so. When he arrived at the center in 2015, he said he would have stopped the world spinning for her. He had slipped into a very dark place and was questioning his legacy. Months later, he had emailed me, seeming to find that thread that stitched him back to life.

He wrote: "There's pure joy in just taking a simple step. I want to spend the rest of my life being present for every moment . . . A life well-lived is given to inspiring others."

I remembered, too, that there was an interior depth to him that one could get lost inside. I had wondered if that depth came from the weight of grief pressing into him so much, it made more room inside of him for others.

On August 16, after the Bible study I led at the truck stop, there was a family emergency, and I left in a hurry to attend to my daughter, who was crying hysterically on the other end of the phone. She was at an animal hospital—her landlady's dog had died in the back of her car. Would I come? I called ISO around nine o'clock, telling him I wasn't sure if or when I might make it. When I arrived at the animal hospital, I held my daughter for a long time, her body quivering, her face swollen, and her skin damp with sweat.

It was after ten before I called ISO back and asked if he wanted to get together or if it was too late. No, he said, he was waiting for me on the upper porch of the inn, sipping some Australian wine. For the first time that night, I noticed the shrill, loud rhythmic sound of the katydids as I arrived at the Deer Head. I uttered a prayer for life-giving conversation, asking God to help me forego the sudden awkwardness I felt in meeting someone on a summer night that I hardly knew. The air, warm and humid, simmered with the scent of jasmine and roses. My eagerness to meet with ISO surprised me, perhaps because it felt like a gift to be called back into someone's life, that two years ago, something mattered of what we had spoken about.

ISO was standing at the top of the stairs, waiting for me. I embraced him as if I had known him for a long time. Something about him made me feel known, or maybe it was my imagination or only my desire. He had gained just enough weight to put him where he needed to be since I had first met him, his beard short and trim, his hair styled and neat—though a little grayer than I remembered. He dressed like a professional after-hours—khaki shorts, a black polo, and sandals. I collapsed into the chair across from his, a bistro table between us. He half-filled a plastic cup with wine. Few words were left in me by now, having taught a study, having been in my office with people coming and going all day, and trying to be a soft place for my daughter to fall. I felt her still leaning into me.

We spoke of small things initially—his flight, his plans the next day to rent a car, where he would be hiking for the next ten days, where he was living now—when his cell phone interrupted. He answered the call. I heard him invite the caller to be a conversation partner, which he later explained was a person with whom one scheduled an in-depth dialogue, at least once a month. Then he invited me to partner with him as well. I agreed.

"So ISO," I asked, swallowing a sip of wine, "did you find what you were 'in search of' on the trail?"

"Did I find what I was looking for? Yes, but don't ask me to define it. Being on the trail was a transformative experience," he said, adding that he had given his marriage another chance, but he wasn't convinced it could succeed; some truth was missing. He was living near his niece and nephew to bond with them, having lived so far away for a dozen years, a decision he had made two years ago while hiking. "The thing is, my niece is at the age when it's difficult to get her to join me at IHOP for a date every month, so I'm coming in a little late in the game. I meet with my nephew to coach him on robotics."

His voice grew more silvery the longer he talked as if his tongue was dipped in moonlight, shedding light on the darkest places of life itself—rejection, reinventing a life, belonging, where, and to whom. He agreed to let me record the conversation.

"You know, there're a lot of people out on the trail with the trail name ISO," he said.

"Really? My question is—can they find what they are in search of if they can't name what they are in pursuit of?" I asked.

"Interesting question. I think they're looking for a purpose beyond survival. People hike the trail during a midlife crisis as a means of escape, but the reality is, you have to deal with everything you're trying to escape while you're out there. I found I was having eighty-hour conversations with myself, all day, every day, and these conversations allowed me to understand that the things I had, my possessions, had no bearing on my happiness. Possessions mean nothing—I had every material thing I needed in my pack: food, a change of clothes, water, a tent. What I needed was a connection, was family." ISO paused to pour more wine into his cup, then took a sip, gazing out into the trees across the street. "I met people on the trail I would never have met otherwise. I met a truck driver who was so happy, a family man. I would've traded everything I had built out of my life in an instant to have what he had. I made in one year what he made in five years. He's a lifelong friend now living here in Pennsylvania. I came to understand what's important and what really makes a person happy."

"So, you found happiness, or maybe the better word is contentment?" I asked.

He hesitated, then asked, "Define what you mean by contentment."

At first, I hesitated. *What did I mean by contentment?* "I mean, are you satisfied with life, is there a settled joy in you, are you aware, awake, do you love life enough?"

"I'm not sure if I have yet," he said.

"When you were hiking two years ago, you were hoping to forgive your spouse for her infidelity. Do you think it possible for anyone to find happiness without forgiving someone who has wounded them so deeply, and I guess that implies forgiving oneself as well?" I asked.

"I guess I'm still struggling with that. I don't think she's confessed to the entire affair. You figure out that after seven years of marriage, you both aren't the same people. She's not who I married. Some find a way to marry each other again and again. I haven't yet," he said, then paused. "I'm missing the companionship part."

"I know the constant ache and throbbing emptiness of divorce," I confessed, "and that awful sense of being abandoned,"

"I'm profoundly lonely at times. I don't have any bandwidth to be involved with anyone right now. I know what it should be like. I'm just not interested, even when I think I might be. I think, for me, there's a fear of rejection that I'm not desirable enough."

I wanted to say to him that he had everything—looks, high intelligence, success, an inquisitive mind, education, an admirable work ethic, the ability to talk intimately, but I held back, feeling as if to say so was somehow too provocative. I was acutely aware of the silence between us as if things were being said and heard. The air felt like pure oxygen.

"When I was a kid," I said, "I found a notecard on my older brother's desk. On the front was the sketch of a naked man squatting in the corner of a room, his head bent over his knees, his long hair spilling over his hands. Underneath him were the words, 'Because I am afraid to love, I am alone.' I've never been able to forget that, even now, so many years later. Maybe we can't discover that we aren't alone until we are alone—do you know what I mean?"

"No, can you say more?"

"I mean, eventually, I found loneliness to be a gift." I felt like I had said too much, but I continued anyway. "I discovered something that Meister Eckhart once wrote, and I've worked hard to cling to it. He was a theologian who lived eight hundred years ago. He said, 'There's a place in the soul where you've never been wounded.'"

He seemed to find some shelter in that quote. His eyes closed around it for a moment. A few cars zoomed by; the katydids turned up the volume.

I realized I had missed this debriefing at the end of the day with a partner over the last several years, this kind of companionship—sipping wine or tea with someone, washing away the sweet and bitter taste of the hours however they were spent.

"Here's what loneliness taught me," I continued. "I've all kinds of ways of avoiding pain. One is to get lost in my work. Another way was to find love quickly again after a failed marriage. I thought I'd grieved my first marriage while I was in it and trying to get out of it, but there's a different kind of mourning once it's over and you aren't living together anymore. I never gave myself over to that kind of sorrow the first time, never really healed, just moved on. I'd never really been alone, and I was scared to death since I had two teenage girls in my care. My dad used to say, don't look back. But, I'm looking back now and looking forward, if that makes any sense." I laughed. "I will say, now almost five years later, the gift of loneliness has been to fully own myself and my life, my passions, my mistakes, my past—all of me, the good, the bad, the ugly. Not easy. It's a lot to deal with."

"Would you be willing to write up something about what you just said about loneliness being a gift and send it to me?" He poured a little more wine into my cup.

"Sure, as long as I can remember what I said," I chuckled. "What I know for sure is that we rarely grow or change without pain and suffering."

Again there was a long pause that I tried not to move through; the silence between us felt sacred. There was no sense of time.

"Not many people know my story," he said. "I entrusted it with only a few, with those who I was sure would honor my story, who would give me unbiased advice. Those with whom I could have an unfettered conversation. All of them are women—why is that?"

"Maybe you were looking to find trust again with women, with one woman. Maybe it was a way back to her, your wife, I mean," I said.

"Maybe."

We talked until after eleven. I stood, and we hugged for a long time. As we embraced, it was as if we knew the wilderness in each other without having walked it together, as if we were mapping some human geography that would locate the place where we are never wounded.

SOLO

*He's filling empty space with the substance of our lives,
confessions of his belly bottom strain, remembrance of
ideas, rehashes of old blowing. He has to blow across
bridges and come back and do it with such infinite
feeling soul-exploratory for the tune of the moment that
everybody knows it's not the tune that counts but IT.*

Jack Kerouac

HIKING IS LIKE JAZZ: IT'S improvisational. It takes time to find
one's rhythm and pace and courage to go solo. When hikers reach
Delaware Water Gap, it's not uncommon to see them hanging out on
the front porch of the Deer Head Inn. Here, jazz greats the likes of
Phil Woods, Rick Chamberlain, and Bill Goodwin continue the inn's
history of passing jazz on to the next generation.

Small tables line the porch that wraps around the white clapboard
inn on two sides. The worn, gray-painted floor slants slightly toward
the road. The second-floor porch offers a view of the Delaware River
and the Gap, or at least it once did at the turn of the twentieth century
when the Gap was one of the most popular vacation spots in the Northeast. Here, hikers charge up their phones, sip a beer, write in their journals, call home while trumpets blow, the piano sings, and saxophones
trill.

Mid-summer, the church hosts Camp Jazz, where thirty-plus teens
lug their instruments and dreams of artistry and fame to Fellowship
House for seven days of intensive jazz immersion. During these days,
I sit in my office as hikers lounge on the grass, listening to the young

musicians play upstairs. The occasional discordant or shrill note startles me from my sermon and hikers from their cell phones.

The atmospherics change at church during Camp Jazz week. It becomes heavy with dreams of greatness, living for one's art, the wildfire that is the creative spirit, a certain madness that can hold a person hostage all his or her life. During lunchtime, the young musicians and their mentors head over to the Deer Head Inn for a boxed meal while they feast on the words and sounds of Phil Woods. Hikers, too, stop in their tracks, throw off their packs as they descend from the trailhead, and collapse into one of the metal chairs outside to listen.

SUMMER 2014, CAMP JAZZ

The famed musician was tethered to an oxygen tank; his arthritic hands clung to his saxophone, his true life support. At eighty-two, Phil Wood's voice was weak, his lungs barely capable of inflating words, yet when he lifted the saxophone to his lips, he played like a full-bodied, full-lunged, young man. Propped on a three-legged stool, the burly man with the bristly gray mustache and cloudy eyes still wore his signature leather fisherman's cap, even in the late July heat.

"Talking is hard, playing is easy," he said to the attentive young audience. "Jazz music—it's the place where strain and relief intersect; it's a relief valve. Ear is your best friend, but you have to have an educated ear. You have to find the note."

The oxygen hissed and flowed like a flute playing in the distance, two notes repeating themselves again and again. Woods's music was smooth, his language gruff, slipping a few expletives into sentences that worked to endear him to a generation where few flinched at such expressions. Years of playing in nightclubs, years of smoking, years of inhaling the secondhand smoke while jazz lovers sucked in his music left his voice raspy and his body diseased. His voice and his music seemingly came from two different places within him.

"Oxygen is nature's amplifier," he said. "It's nature's way of saying you've played too many effing notes."

The students listened, most with their mouths agape, to the four-time Grammy Award winner. They knew they were in the company of greatness.

He continued, "It's important to be kind, but difficult. I try to maintain my sweet disposition." Everyone laughed. He told them the arts exploded after World War II and tacked on a shortened version of his oral biography—how he had played with the best and the famous: Benny Goodman, Buddy Rich, Quincy Jones, Dizzy Gillespie, and Billy Joel; how in 2007, he was named a Jazz Master by the National Endowment for the Arts.

The students could see that this famed saxophonist was dying, slowly, in front of them. Fourteen months later, he would blow his horn for the last time.

What they came for, one young man had dared to ask: "What makes a musician rise to greatness?" He swung his long dark bangs away from his eyes like a cool cat, as jazz musicians were often called.

"Be the best player in the world. What makes for greatness? One thing. Practice, practice, practice, be good, learn the craft, play twenty-six hours a day for twenty years. Do the mathematics. Do you have the fire? Bring something special. You've got to play truth. Good musicians need to hear the truth. You've got to play truth." His speech halted like a deliberate musical rest.

I noticed the microphone shaking in his hand, and when he tilted his head toward my direction that he had a Breathe-Rite bandage across his nose. He was wearing socks that were once white, black corduroy slippers, jeans, and a stretched-out gray tee shirt. It seemed to me that all he cared about was music.

"Play truth. Play your note, sing your song—whatever it may be—only make it real." As I looked out the long, wavy-glass window that was half open, I saw a few hikers looking stunned by what they heard as if this is what they had been doing, or trying to do, on their 2,200-mile hike.

"You have to find a community that cares about jazz. The Gap is a watering hole for jazz musicians. A whole bunch of cats lived here. You've got to do your scales fifty times a day. You have to ask yourself, what is the intent of the lyricist? How to play rests. I shape solos around my afflictions. There's more silence in my music. I need more space."

He paused to inhale, then added: "Don't smoke nothin'."

The students stuffed their gaping mouths with sandwiches.

"If you're married and you're a working musician, you have responsibilities. You'll be working at home, or you're on the road. These are the needs of the soul and heart—you have to juggle."

A hiker in full gear entered the inn. His long blond dreadlocks were pulled back into a ponytail, and he had his hiking poles looped around one wrist. He asked the owner, Denny, a dead lookalike for Nick Nolte, if this was the hostel? Denny told him the center is next door, at the church, up the steep driveway. I watched him leave the way he came and I said nothing, to my shame. But I was trapped inside the interrupted silence.

"Become a cultured human being. Get to know other artists. Listen to Beethoven, operas, symphonies. Give up looking for the magic reed or sax or strap."

Between his words, you could hear the clang of soda cans and plastic water bottles opened, tipped, then placed back down on the table, along with the occasional crinkling of saran wrap and foil. The place smelled of cold cuts. Students shuffled their feet, but never their eyes away from Phil as he lifted his saxophone to his wetted lips and played.

He blew that horn. Notes like stained glass shattered the air, and colors fell everywhere, letting in light and dark. Scales of grace and hurt, cadences of grief and joy rushed into the room, into me, and scraped away the thin layer of time where so much hid beneath. The music exposed memories—the emptiness of my body when my son was born, the fullness of my arms as I held him for the first time. That sax cried, I swore it cried, and the sounds came from me even though no one else could hear them.

Phil appeared winded after playing for a few long minutes. He placed the saxophone down in its stand—but the music was still there, in the atmosphere, inside us. Slouching backward, he expanded his chest. Color came back into his ashen face.

A moment later, he asked the ultimate question: "Ask yourself, what do I want more than music and fill in the blank. If you want anything more than this"—he lifted up his saxophone, his life support—"then follow that."

Jazz was his conscience, his guiding light, his breath—all he ever wanted. I glanced outside to see a half-dozen hikers staring into the space jazz had opened. Phil had said he needed more silence in his music. I wondered if there wasn't some inaudible music, at least inaudible to others, that underscored every step a hiker took on the trail—music they heard and that kept them going. Was it heard in the aria of stars and darkness, the thump of things that startle in the night, the whisper of distant water, the murmur of wind? Or maybe it was the sound of one's panting, the grunt and groan of great effort, the beat of feet on the ground.

That madness, that inner fire that made Phil Woods play his saxophone a million times, that flame for greatness that burns in the young, is the same. It sends the old and young alike into the wilderness to walk thousands of miles, scramble up fallen rocks, and wade across frigid streams. Feet against the earth like a match striking stone stirs, sparks, and stokes the divine fire within us all, like jazz itself.

BRAND EQUITY

What you see and what you hear depends a great deal on where you are standing. It also depends on what sort of person you are.

C.S. Lewis

I STARED INTO THE FIERY TREES— the glowing embers of maple leaves, the slow-burning yellow flames of birch, the sycamore's blaze of orange. I always thought of Moses this time of year, out minding his own business, when he stumbled upon a burning bush, then heard God's voice calling out of the contained inferno to deliver his people. It felt as if every ignited tree was a wilderness in itself, crying out to redeem me. The burnt leaves crumbled, like ashes, to the ground. The skies were silent, the earth still, yet the mid-summer scent clung to the air, as did the warmth that seemed to produce an abundant crop of southbound hikers.

Sparks and Extraordinary arrived toward the end of October, a few days after Determined, Laughter, and Kitty had left. Also in the center was a married couple, who was packing up to depart when I walked in. The couple had sold everything they owned, including their house. They were from New England, looked to be in their thirties, and had no children. Having abandoned their careers before embarking on the AT, they were leaving to be with friends on the West Coast. When I asked them why they had both quit their well-paying careers—one as an engineer and the other as a chemist—both said they had wanted to do what was meaningful in their lives. They had ventured onto the AT to find some clarity on what that meant for them.

"Everyone's walking the trail to work through something," the husband-engineer said. "To be human is to be working through, and toward, something. The conversations you have with others are as much about what the trail experience is about as hiking is."

"We're giving ourselves time to reprioritize our lives. We want to do something inspirational for us," said the wife-chemist. "We aren't going back to our old lives. We're moving on to the next thing, whatever the next thing may be. We're giving ourselves time to reconnect with old friends and family."

When asked what conclusions they had come to, having hiked side-by-side over a thousand miles to arrive here, the husband said he wanted to be a sustainability consultant to industries to reduce their carbon footprint. The wife said she wanted to go in the direction of ecology and considered building a tiny home community. Our conversation ended when a woman came through the door to take them to the airport.

I turned toward Extraordinary, a thirty-one-year-old who stood about five feet, eight inches tall with long, blonde hair woven into a loose side braid, steel-blue eyes, a pink complexion, and a quick tongue. She was preparing to hike solo later that morning, leaving Sparks behind due to an ankle injury. They were going to meet up in a day or two if Sparks could hitch a ride to Wind Gap, about sixteen miles south.

"Two years ago, I went to Vietnam by myself with no particular plan in mind," Extraordinary said. Her words were like iron—strong, unbending, bold. "I didn't know what I was going to do when I got there, but I found my way to an orphanage run by Franciscan brothers, and I worked there for a year. I went with one of the brothers to visit his village where there was no electricity or phones or anything, and I slipped on a wet floor and broke my leg in eight places. There was no doctor, no hospital. One of the village men made me a splint out of bamboo; then, I had to board a bus and ride for eight hours before getting to a hospital in Hanoi. I can't even begin to tell you how much pain I was in. A doctor who was serving Doctors Without Borders did emergency surgery, and I walked around in a cast for a couple of months. So when I say that I learned I could face anything and take care of myself, I did."

"It took me until my thirties before I traveled by myself," I said. "My first overseas assignment as a journalist was to Ireland, writing about a 110-mile horse trek through Connemara. I had only three horse-riding lessons under my belt. Shortly after, I flew to Saudi Arabia with the U.S. Air Force for an assignment on Desert Storm. I was scared to death that I would die during both assignments, and I almost did."

"I grew up with a single dad who taught me to fear no one and nothing," Extraordinary said. "I started at Princeton University in a master's program when I got back from Vietnam, and I was in a cast, hobbling around with crutches my first semester. Now that was hard!" As she strolled around the center, collecting her gear and placing items into or near her backpack, she seemed to repeatedly snag her right foot on one of the pack's straps and stumble.

Sparks looked at me and said, "Yeah, she took a couple of face plants on the trail. I had to pull her up by the straps of her backpack." Sparks was the quieter of the two. She stood about five-foot-two and cut a slender silhouette. Having shaved her head before starting the trail in early July, her hair had grown into a stylish pixie cut. It was difficult not to stare at the greenish-blue color she had dyed it; the shade matched her eyes. There was timidity in her eyes and her body as if she were walking too close to an unseen edge and had to protect herself from falling.

"How about you, Sparks? How's it been on the trail for you before you started to hike with Extraordinary?" I asked.

"I grew up full of fear in an ultra-conservative Christian home. I was afraid of the world and everybody in it. I was homeschooled until I went away to college. Have you ever heard of the 'True Love Waits' movement?'"

"No, I can't say I have," I said.

"It's a movement that expects young men and women to marry as innocents. My very first kiss was at the altar during my wedding. I was twenty-one," she said.

"And how was that, experiencing your first kiss on your wedding day, in front of an audience?" I asked.

"It was terrible."

"Then I can't imagine how your wedding night must have been for you," I said.

"It was traumatic," Sparks said. "I was married for seven years and fell deeper and deeper into depression. Last year I attempted suicide. We're divorced now."

I admired her forthrightness. Maybe that was a gift of the trail—if a person doesn't walk away from the things that have broken them, they walk toward them.

"I was hospitalized after my attempt," she continued. "One thing the trail's taught me is to watch for the white blazes; they're right in front of you. All I need to do hiking, and in life, is to look for the next white rectangle, take one step at a time."

"Please don't feel you have to answer this question," I said with a fair amount of trepidation, "but can you tell me about your depression?"

"My depression was nothing new—I had struggled with it all my life. My unsatisfying, failing marriage only deepened it," Sparks said.

"I imagine telling your parents was particularly difficult," I said.

"It was, but they've been supportive, to my surprise, really. I think my mom has suffered depression all of her life. When I was young, she'd just tell me I was a bad kid, or I needed to try harder, or pray harder, trust God more when I was depressed. My ex was doing a lot of crazy stuff like gaslighting, but I was kind of used to that since my mom had always done that too. One of my siblings attempted suicide, as well."

Maybe that was the edge she was desperately trying not to fall from, into emptiness.

"I like being on my own out here on the trail, meeting people. Where I'm from in the South, women are trained to be nice, even when they aren't," she continued.

"I learned I didn't have to be nice to everyone," Extraordinary chimed in. "My dad's an adventurous man. He lived in many countries, and I grew up traveling around the world."

"Traveling, living among different cultures, does change how you view the world, and it takes away the fear of the other," I said.

"Definitely," Extraordinary said. "When I was thirteen, I went to live with my dad in London. I think my mom's bipolar, although she was never officially diagnosed. Last year was the year of misfortune for me. After breaking my leg, then going to Princeton, I ended up hospitalized and diagnosed with bipolar disorder. I needed a reset, a massive challenge for body, mind, and spirit—so I'm hiking. The trail represents all that."

If there was a common theme as to why people hit the AT, perhaps it's just that—to reset or renew. For some, it's an act of resistance. What they seek is their path.

"I had always managed myself before I was hospitalized," Extraordinary continued. "If people see things in black and white, people with bipolar see everything in Technicolor. I worried that when I was out on the trail and being alone and so active, it would be worse, but I have faith in myself again. I needed to get back to basics."

The phrase "faith in myself" kept running through my head. It was clear that the women had bonded through the shared experience of being hospitalized for their various conditions and hiking the trail for a new sense of direction.

"My brand equity for doing this is off the charts. I work with men, only men in my field, and when they heard I was hiking the AT all by myself, roughing it, my employability, my self-stock, skyrocketed."

"Really?" I asked.

"The men I work with all married princesses, you know, materialistic women. The men would love to do what I'm doing, but they can't; they have too many responsibilities. They idealize what I'm doing, and they idealize me for doing it," Extraordinary said.

The AT is part-romance, especially for those who only dream of finding themselves lost in the wilderness, who imagine waking up outdoors, breathing in the stars all night. To call oneself adventurous, risk the loss of all material things, feel how the earth enters one's bones through the soles of one's feet, and confront one's demons alone has a cost that few are willing to pay. Though, the dividends last a lifetime for those who do it, not the least being belief in oneself. Self-stock, brand equity, idealization—for Extraordinary, these were the dividends for completing the trail. Gone were the labels she had worn willingly or unwillingly.

With birth names and addresses unknown, hikers leave their predictable, organized lives to wander an unpredictable, rugged paradise. Somewhere along the way, they pass an invisible divide, somewhere between the beginning and the end of their trek, a place different for each one. Bruises, blisters, aches, and pains are all part of the necessary severing from the life lived before this exodus. Such was essential to break the hold of safety and its slavery, freeing the pilgrim spirit—to search for, or recover, some excellence lost along the way.

Extraordinary finished pressing fresh supplies deep into her pack. As she lifted the pack to her shoulders, she snagged her foot once again on the loose strap but caught herself before face-planting on the carpet tiles.

BROKEBACK

Jesus replied, "Go back and report to John what you hear and see: The blind receive sight, the lame walk, the lepers are cleansed, the deaf hear, the dead are raised, and good news is preached to the poor. Blessed is the one who does not fall away on account of Me."

Matthew 11:5
Berean Study Bible

THEY CALLED HIM BROKEBACK, NAMED for an injury he had suffered two years earlier when he fractured his neck and had undergone surgery to remove two vertebrae. A surgery so risky that it was nearly miraculous he didn't end up as a paraplegic, although he suffered nerve damage. Brokeback was northbound, even though it was mid-August, having started in Georgia on April 9.

"I'm not running a race," he said. "I'm walking slow, at my pace. With every step, I'm full of gratitude that I can walk at all." He stretched out his arms to show me his fingers, how they trembled and spasmed as a result of his damaged nerves. "I used to be in the catering business; now I can't even cut an onion."

Brokeback was a joyous sort. He had a Southern accent, a gravelly smoker's voice from the sound of it. Slight of build, he was thin from all the miles he had walked. In his late forties, he looked as if he had battled alcoholism and aged prematurely, skin slack for his years. Addiction draws its signature, impressing its hollow scribble of lost days and dreams upon the most beautiful body and Christ-starved face, I thought.

Throughout our conversation, he would periodically lift his arms, spread out his quaking limbs, and shout, "Glory to God!" Praise was irrepressible in him, rushing out of him as if all that was lost was nothing compared to what he had gained.

He was sitting on one of the leather couches in the center on this unspeakably humid morning, at least for me, a northeasterner. The odor of hikers was equally unbearable; I forced myself to breathe it all in, along with the nearly stagnant breeze that blew in from time to time through the window as I sat in the direction of the fan so I wouldn't die from heatstroke or suffocation.

Wearing a stained t-shirt, khaki-colored nylon shorts, and a camouflage fishing hat, half of Brokeback's face was shadowed. His chin-length hair was dark, wavy, and a little scraggly, like his untrimmed beard. I couldn't see the color of his eyes.

"How did you injure yourself?" I asked.

"I was wearing flip-flops. It was raining outside, and I took a horrible spill. It took me two years to learn to walk again—it was a long struggle. I'm on disability now. If my cord had been snipped, it would have been all over. They put in rods, they put me on pain pills. When they started to wean me off of them there pills, I started drinkin' off the pain. I struggled with addiction most of my life, but I'd never had a big drug problem until after surgery. Booze had always been my problem, though. I couldn't sleep more than a couple of hours without vodka to put me back to sleep again."

He had entered a veteran's hospital back home in Florida for rehabilitation from alcohol abuse a year ago. When asked by the staff if seven days of detox would be enough, he said he had a big bottle of vodka waiting for him when he got back home.

"I started to feel worthless; I had never been depressed in my life, and I went down. I always had faith in God, always. One day, I decided to change my life."

Brokeback voluntarily enrolled in a ninety-day residential program called *Jesus Is*, located in his home state. Gone were his vodka, his pills. Remaining was all the hurt, insomnia, and depression. He hadn't slept in a year without pain.

"I started to pray at night when I couldn't sleep. I prayed through my suffering, my agony, my hopelessness, my worthlessness. In time, I started to sleep again."

Jesus Is calls itself "A spiritual hospital for God's most hurting sheep. A place where real people with real problems meet a real God and get really delivered." The ministry began over thirty years ago when Jim and Gloria Adams lost their oldest son due to an accident. It was at their son's funeral that Jim heard God speak to him.

According to the ministry's website, everything changed at that moment in Jim Adams's life. He closed his business and donated its building and property to the "work of the Lord." That same building now houses forty men who come for deliverance from their addictions. The criteria for who comes for rehabilitation?

"We can only help those who will make a firm commitment to God to remain with us for ninety days and follow the rules. However, those who are serious and make a firm commitment are really able to turn their lives around and experience the new beginning that is characterized by a closer relationship with God, faith, prayer, and service to others. The facility's eighteen acres are called 'Holy Ground.'"

"If I'd seen what I saw any earlier than when I did, I would have walked out of there."

"What did you see?" I asked.

"There was speaking in tongues, people being slain in the spirit. I had nothing in my experience of Catholicism to prepare me for that, but I found God there as I had never before found God," he said, shaking his head side to side. "While I was there, I had a vision of myself hiking the Appalachian Trail. I've been walking with a few hikers who are trying to stay straight and sober; I'm trying to help them by being there with them. Sometimes I get so filled up, I can't help but stop and lift my arms and praise God out loud." And sure enough, he lifted his arms and praised God out loud again. "People see me, and they think I'm nuts, but I can't help but do otherwise."

Tears slipped down his cheeks like streams from a deep invisible river that ran through him.

"Until I was thirteen, I believed my stepfather was my father. Then my real father showed up. It was all very confusing because I had heard nothing but horror stories about him. It took a long time to bond with him," Brokeback continued. "I never really got to know my father throughout the years, but he showed up at Harper's Ferry and bought me gear for the trail, took me to dinner, got me stuff. He said it was for all the times he wasn't there for my birthday." Tears spotted his shorts. "I think he was looking for redemption."

Redemption—such an all-embracing word, I thought.

"I was baptized on Christmas day," he said. "I don't know how to explain it, but it really did make a difference in me. I'm not the fastest on the trail. I almost didn't make it past the first day because I had so much pain carrying my gear, with the strain on my back and neck. I can't do it without your help, Lord," he said, arms reaching up, eyes cast to the ceiling as if the ceiling were the sky, and as if Jesus were right there between us. "I can't stop crying while I'm talking to you." He stood up and headed toward the door, his back bent over for a short distance before straightening up.

I wondered if his tears were partly baptismal waters.

TRAIL OF TEARS

I've cried, and you'd think I'd be better for it, but the sadness just sleeps, and it stays in my spine the rest of my life.

Conor Oberst

NAMES. IT'S HOW WE KNOW ourselves and how others know us. Hikers are named by other hikers mostly, usually by something that distinguishes that person. For example, a young man was called Radio for lugging an eight-inch transistor radio he tied to the back of his pack. I couldn't figure out why anyone would want music blaring while traveling the wilderness unless it was thought to keep wild things away, including one's untamed thoughts.

Another hiker, about fifty years old, told me his trail name was "Two Weeks, Three Days."

"How'd you get that name?" I asked.

"That's how long my wife said I would last on the trail," he answered.

Map Quest, Vanilla Thunder, Crusty Goat, Rivet, Skywalker, Fire Man, Xena, Treasure Hunter, and Late Start are only a few such trail names. Short Stop earned his name for having to rest every few steps to catch his breath. We talked after one of the potluck hikers dinners during my first summer there.

What most didn't know about Short Stop was why he, in his late sixties, was driven to hike the AT for the second time in three years. He appeared older than he was. His skin was a bit ashen as if something had burned out in him. It was the look of both age and sorrow, the look of someone who learned firsthand that no one is fireproof.

His hair was leaden-colored and thin, and he sported a sparse white beard. His eyes looked wrung of color. He was so soft-spoken, even as he explained that he had been angry at God. His story began when his grandson had been diagnosed with pediatric cancer on his third birthday.

"They did the surgery, and the doctors were convinced that they got all of the tumor attached to his spine, but they said they couldn't be absolutely sure they got it all. They strongly recommended chemotherapy and the full protocol. Chemo destroyed his heart. Five months later, he died. His heart just gave up."

He paused to catch his breath as if he was walking up a steep hill. People around us began to disperse. Hikers were sent back to the center with all the leftover food. We were alone.

"The autopsy showed no trace of cancer; the chemo killed him. He was diagnosed in October of 2007 and died in April the following year. I tried support groups and everything; I just couldn't find my new normal. About six months later, I followed my daily routine—get up, get dressed, get in the car, and drive all day to avoid being anywhere. One day I found myself in Smoky Mountains State Park, Case Cove Loop Road, in early October. The leaves were turning color, and I was driving about five miles-per-hour when I was halfway around the loop, and I saw all these cars pulled over at a parking area. I pulled in and followed the people who were getting out of their cars and walked into the woods. I walked two-point-four miles to the waterfalls and two-point-four miles back. In those nearly five miles, I talked to about fifty people. People were talking to each other. When I got back to the car, it dawned on me that this was the best I had felt in six months."

Strangers, conversation, movement; no one knew of this grandfather's loss, nor of the gravity of his grief, as they had talked and walked with him. Maybe it was the exertion or reaching out or the wildness of the park that sparked healing in him.

"A few days later, I did another trail, then another, and then the Kant, and now I'm hooked. I joined a hiking group and ended up hiking all the trails of the Smokies three times."

He paused. "The day my grandson died, my son-in-law had called to tell me that my grandson was dying. I got up early in the morning to drive up to Virginia. By the time I got to Roanoke, about ten o'clock, my son-in-law had called me. He told me to pull over. He said that the doctors sedated my grandson and put him on a breathing tube. His heart stopped thirty minutes later."

A flash flood came in his eyes, fast and furious. He bit his lower lip as if to hold it back. What passed between us in the next minute was a kind of silent thunderstorm that rattled us both.

I remembered my son when he was three years old, the feel of his fast-beating heart against me when I picked him up and carried him inside after running around the yard, and how he'd sing upstairs in his bedroom while he played with Legos or army men for hours, his feet folded under his legs. I felt the ache of loss, the emptiness of arms, and the anger of innocence stolen. It was impossible to shake off.

"In 2012, I started on the Appalachian Trail in January. I was all alone. One day, I was in a shelter during a winter storm. No one else was there. I went days without seeing anybody. Some people are afraid to be alone when they're grieving; you know what I mean?"

I nodded. "It can be terrifying," I said as I recalled my own experiences of grief—the panic attacks, feeling that I was untethered and drifting in a sea of tsunamis; how no matter whose hand was extended or how far, I couldn't reach it. I couldn't be pulled back.

"God and I talked a lot. I cried, I screamed at Him," he went on. "There were no interruptions—cell phones didn't work—it was just me and the wilderness and God. I got over being angry with God—I realized there are so many things we can't control. It's about how you react to things. This is the hardest thing I've ever been through. I came to understand that God isn't the one who gave us cancer."

Or take it away, I wanted to say.

Short Stop continued, "I see my daughter doing things now she would've never done before. She's involved with others and with her faith. She adopted a biracial girl whose mother and father were addicts and whose father's in jail. My daughter was in the delivery room, and here she's with this beautiful daughter. My daughter's involved with charitable organizations, including 46, an organization of mothers who race for pediatric cancer research and shave their heads every year. They've raised over a million dollars. The name 46 is for how many children are diagnosed with pediatric cancer every day."

After completing the trail in 2012, Short Stop returned two years later as a designated chaplain on the AT with the United Methodist Church. A patch on his backpack looked more like a Boy Scout merit badge only with "Chaplain" embossed across it. His job, as he saw it, was to offer encouragement to others, to stay with the injured until help arrived, to listen as young people sought for signs along the way as to what to do with their lives. The patch drew as many people as it repelled.

By the time we finished talking, the moon shone, and the air sang with hidden life. It was as if the night smelled of tears; maybe it was the scent of the river that flowed nearby, somehow magnified in the blue-back skies.

"Time for me to turn in. Hikers sleep by the moon and rise by the sun," he said, inching himself slowly off the picnic bench, standing and stretching the stiffness from his spine and legs.

As I reached out to hug him, I asked, "What was your grandson's name?"

"Walker," he said.

GIRLS ON THE TRAIL

Men are afraid that women will laugh at them. Women are afraid that men will kill them.

Margaret Atwood

❝❙ HAVE NO FEAR ANYMORE," SAID Determined, a female hiker who had been trekking sections of the AT for most of her life. "I used to sit in my truck at a trailhead and wait for everyone to leave before I would dash out of my truck and hike the trail by myself."

It was October, and the hikers had dwindled from dozens to about four or six each day; most were southbound, flip-flopping, or section-hiking. The center itself had aired out somewhat with the cooler temperatures, and fresh air flowed in from the open window since it was warm enough, sometimes even hot, during the fall of 2017. It felt like the space itself needed a rest from accommodating over thirteen hundred hikers already that year as if its arms were tired from holding them all. Even the walls seemed to sigh and sag.

I couldn't tell how old Determined was. She seemed to have the confidence of a woman in her forties, but she looked to be somewhere in her thirties. She had a childless figure—narrow-hipped, perky breasts, shallow-boned—at least that's how I saw it compared to my own birth-marked body. I always thought that there's something about mothers' bodies. It's as if they are broken open not only in the birthing of a child, but the bodies remain open and forever vulnerable. I don't know if childless women feel the same since I became a mother at twenty-two.

Determined's eyes were the color of the Delaware River after a rainstorm—a rich sienna hue full of currents that swirled the more she talked about the trials of being a girl on the trail. She flipped her long, shiny dark hair off her shoulders as she spoke as if to draw an exclamation point as she tilted forward, toying with her pack, preparing to leave.

Two other women, Laughter and Kitty, were in the center that morning. Each had hiked solo many miles, but they had found each other a distance back and had stayed together over the last week. Laughter had brought along her docile Australian Shepherd, Blue, for company and protection. Blue roamed between us that morning, receiving a dose of affection from one before moving to the next. He could never get enough. David Childs was there in the center too, helping out as usual.

"I've learned to walk alone," Determined continued. "I've walked with five different guys, and every one of them got injured on day two and had to get off the trail. And none of them could keep up with me. I'd be waiting like an hour for them to meet up with me. I told myself I had to get over my fear. Women I met on the trail would tell me—don't tell guys your real name or where you're from; be as vague as possible. Set up camp away from the others, sleep on the other side of a berm, and don't light a campfire. Don't give any information. Don't stay in the shelters, don't party with locals or those who are drinking," she said, then laughed.

Listening to Determined, I thought men and women exist in vastly different worlds, even though both are immersed in the same physical surroundings. It didn't matter where they were, be it in the woods or on the streets amid skyscrapers. Their inner geography was different— their fears seemed miles apart.

Determined, the oldest among the female trinity, said: "I start to get creeped out when a man asks me all kinds of questions, like 'Where did you stay last night? Where are you staying tonight? Are there people behind you? Are you going north or south? Do you think you're going to make it?' My favorite questions are, 'Are you sure you should be out here?' and, 'Are you by yourself?'"

"Yeah, that would make me a bit nervous," I chimed in.

"Once, when I was alone on the trail and taking a break at a shelter in the middle of an afternoon, a guy going the opposite direction, a day hiker, sees me, turns around, walks in and says, 'I'm a preacher in town.'" She lowered her voice to imitate the man. "He kept telling me how much I should trust him because he's a preacher, that people knew him. I started feeling *really* uncomfortable. Then he starts taking a bunch of photos of the shelter, and he's getting progressively closer and closer to me with his camera, so I pull out my camera, and I take photos and step away from him. For the next three miles, I hike with my knife dangling around my neck."

I guessed fearlessness has its limits. I wondered if banishing one fear helped to banish other fears in her life. Maybe she learned as I had long ago that the only way to overcome any fear is to confront it, move through it, then pass it.

Laughter interjected that Determined carried a spot tracker on her pack that pings every ten minutes to pinpoint her location in case she is lost or injured so that her family or a search team knew where to find her. In her early twenties, Laughter was a slight young woman, with one side of her head shorn and the other with a flop turquoise-colored hair.

"I had attempted the trail before," Laughter said, "but I started up with a party bubble. I felt protected in the group. There was a lot of comfort in that. We developed a kind of pack mentality; we had a *tramily*—a trail family." She was attempting to walk alone this time, since the party bubble bursts at the end of every July, when many decide they have to go off trail as they would never make it to Katahdin on time.

The catalyst for the entire conversation was a confrontation that had happened the night before. We had begun locking the center because days earlier, someone had walked in and stolen a seventy-two-year-old hiker's blanket, pillow, and ski mask while a funeral service was held in the upstairs sanctuary. The hiker was setting out to walk a hundred-mile section of the trail even though he suffered Parkinson's Disease. Also stolen was a handmade quilt that had been donated to the church years ago. We assumed a person without a home had taken the blankets to stay warm as the temperatures were falling during the night.

Determined told us that when she and the other two women had arrived at the church, she saw a dented silver car in the parking lot, and she went into the Fellowship House behind the church, looking for someone to unlock the center door.

"A man emerged from somewhere inside," she said. "I don't even know where he came from, but there was no one else there. I thought maybe he'd have a key to the center, but there was something off about him. A little later, he drove his car down to the center while we were waiting for David. The guy was almost blocking the door, and he remarked about the dog. He said how he needed to be loved and how maybe the dog would love him. He didn't feel safe to me."

I asked her for a physical description of the man. Two weeks earlier, we'd had another complaint about a man in a dented silver car. I had called the police and kept an eye out for him, as he was told not to be on church property. She described him as having a shaved head and a tattoo of some sort on the back of his neck. David explained that on Sunday nights, AA meets in Fellowship House, and about an hour and a half before the meeting starts, someone comes in to set up the coffee.

"When I came last night to unlock the center and saw him there, I know I was a bit abrupt with him," David said as if apologizing. "I didn't get a good look at him since it was dark."

I added, "We've had a few unnerving situations here the last couple of weeks. Two weeks ago, a young woman hiker texted me that there was a strange old guy in the center. She was alone. I told her to take a photo of him and send it to me without being too obvious. The man was tall and gaunt, with a white beard and sunken eyes. It turns out the guy was known around town, a homeless person who suffered some mental illness. He had taken a shower and was walking around naked when she came in. Now that's a greeting never to be forgotten!"

The women seemed anxious to head out, and armed with new information, David and I jumped into my truck and started to scout the streets, the parking lots, and the trailhead for a dented silver car with a Pennsylvania license plate. No luck. Later that afternoon, I went into town and purchased a keypad lock so that hikers had one security element between them and the world when they came to the center. We'd have to question the hikers who called to decide whether they were legit or not, asking things like, where are they hiking from? Where did they stay last night? All the questions that guys asked the girls out on the trail. There was an irony to that.

The day, like the season, darkened as if it would rain, but the fall drought continued. It seemed to me that the center itself needed to go into hibernation, sleep for a season, forget all the ways it could not keep its guests completely safe from thieves and intruders, or from those hungry and thirsty for something other than food.

VISION QUEST

*Not till we are lost, in other words, not till we have lost
the world, do we begin to find ourselves.*

Henry David Thoreau

J UST AS NATIVE AMERICANS HAVE vision quest, the Hindus have
two stages in a man's life after his duty as a householder comes
to an end. First, he becomes a hermit in retreat, renouncing all plea-
sures, retiring from social and professional life, leaving home to live
in a forest hut. He spends his time in prayer. The next and final stage
occurs when he becomes a wandering ascetic, utterly devoted to God,
homeless, with no attachment to the earth, desires or fears, duties, or
responsibilities. He seeks moksha, or salvation, being released from
the circle of birth, death, and rebirth.

The rest of us have the trail.

G-Walker was on a vision quest, like other older hikers. Lanky,
over six feet tall, and balding at his head's crown, he looked to be in
his mid-sixties, even though he had not a strand of gray hair. He was
cleanly shaven—an unusual sight on the AT.

I found him sitting outside the center in one of the green plastic
Adirondack chairs, conversing with other hikers on a hot June afternoon, his long legs crossed at a wide angle. He had a smooth tenor
voice, a large well-practiced laugh, and an openness to him as if he had
spent his professional life depending upon his charisma.

He had hiked over ten miles that day, and he was looking forward
to the church's Thursday night potluck feast. Word travels fast on the
trail. Described as a hot dog dinner in the AT guidebooks, it had be-

come known as a weekly feast, starting in June and running through the end of August. It was the fourth one so far this summer. The church was back in full swing, setting up the back porch of Fellowship House, wiping down over a dozen long tables and their benches, igniting the grill, and arranging the covered dishes—salads, spaghetti, fried chicken, shrimp, bread, corn pudding, among other offerings.

G-Walker had named himself, he told me. The G stood for the first letter of his name—or maybe it was for "God" since he had recently retired after decades of serving as the pastor of a large church in New England. That explained his poise and gregariousness, I thought, as I settled into a chair next to him.

Four-year-old Aliyah, David's granddaughter, was dancing in the driveway, all dressed up in a blue *Frozen* princess gown singing "Let it Go," a good theme song for the trail, I mused.

"I was a minister of a large congregation, a senior pastor, in a well-known church," he said. "It had thousands of members."

"What was the most difficult part of ministry for you?" I asked.

He shifted in his seat, stared out into inner space, then said, "Arrogance."

"Arrogance?" I echoed.

"I had a staff of four pastors beneath me, and I found myself being antagonistic toward the end. I found myself acting in a way that I didn't like, more adversarial. I knew it was time for me to retire. I left in March, and I've been walking ever since. Thought it was a good idea after reading the book *Wild*. Have you read it?" he asked me.

"I haven't finished reading it. It seems like it's been the impetus for many walking the AT this summer." The book, written by Cheryl Strayed, chronicles her hike on the Pacific Crest Trail from the Mojave Desert through California, Oregon, to Washington State, when she was twenty-two. Broken by her mother's death, she destroyed her marriage, became addicted to heroin, and took to the trail to heal herself.

"I realized when I was reading it how the entire book was about grieving, about unpacking grief."

"Are you grieving?" I asked.

He looked at me, startled as if my question had slapped me across the face.

"No, no, no," he insisted. Each "no" a little louder than the one before.

"You said you had just retired. Isn't there always some grieving associated with leaving behind a career you spent your entire life in? I don't mean it isn't a joyous rite of passage, but there has to be some grieving too."

"You know, I never thought about it until you said it. Maybe I am grieving. Maybe I am."

I left him shortly afterward to help with dinner preparations.

On the following Sunday morning, he attended worship. Before the first hymn, he stood up, donned in his hiker garb—dark nylon shorts, a dingy shirt that had once been white. "I just want to thank you," he said to the congregation. "This is a wonderful ministry to hikers, and I am well aware of what goes into this. It isn't easy, and it demands a lot of the church, so thank you."

Once a minister, always a minister.

Seven months after G-Walker came and went, I almost ran over a man on a cold wintry January afternoon with freezing rain pelting my car. He was in my blind spot as I backed up in the church parking lot. I slammed on the brakes before nearly flattening him. Startled and a bit concerned as I was alone at the church, I clutched the small canister of pepper spray that dangled from my keychain. I rolled down my window and apologized for not seeing him.

He saw me, he said, and maneuvered around me.

"Jacque," he said, reaching his hand into the car for me to shake. He was slender and looked to be in his late fifties. His French-Canadian accent was an invitation to travel without having to move, the way words curled around his tongue.

"Pastor Sherry." I reached out and shook his hand.

"I'm going to be hiking the Appalachian Trail this spring, and I am mapping my course. I wanted to know if I could leave insulin here in March so that I don't have to carry it with me."

I noticed he was carrying a small blue pouch in his left hand with the staff of Hermes embossed upon it. I turned off the ignition, walked with him down to the center, unlocked it, and gave him a tour.

Jacque walked around, checked out the bunk room, shower and bathroom. He was wearing hiker pants and open sandals with socks on, a thin layer against the day's wet chill.

"I'm going to start on March ninth, and I just wanted to make sure I could store my insulin at the church. I'll be bringing about eighty syringes to leave in the freezer, with your permission. I take about eight shots a day."

I ran my eyes up and down the man, an unlikely candidate for diabetes from his appearance.

"I'm traveling up and down the trail by car to see where I can store my insulin along the way." He paused, then offered: "I stayed here in 1978 when the hostel first opened. I walked the AT then to figure out whether to become a child care worker or a teacher. In Canada, a child care worker works with troubled youth. I was nineteen then."

"The trail helped you decide?"

"Yes. Maybe it's just the clarity that comes when there is nothing else to focus on. I walked the trail again when I was thirty-one, trying to decide whether to marry my wife, Denise. When I finished the trail, I married her."

"Why are you walking the trail this time?" I asked.

"I have to make a decision. I separated from my wife recently after nineteen years. I have to decide as to whether or not I will care for myself. I want to hike without taking my insulin, but I need to know it's there for me if I need it. I want to see if I can heal myself, if I will need it if I am hiking miles every day."

I did a quick calculation in my head. Six months equals approximately a hundred and eighty days, times eight insulin shots insulin a day, equals fourteen hundred and forty doses he'd have to lug if he couldn't deposit the supply up and down the trail. I wondered how much that would weigh and how much space that would take up in his pack.

"Of course, you can store as much as you need to here. We have two refrigerators, and we can make space."

Jacque hugged me goodbye.

He left a supply of insulin in the outside refrigerator in March and came through in July when I was on vacation. I never found out if walking miles every day made him less dependent on insulin, but knowing he had made it this far was comforting.

Maybe all he needed, like G-Walker, I thought, was a vision for this half of life now that he was alone, retired, dependent upon insulin to live, knowing what he hadn't known so well when he was young—that his days were numbered. Maybe he was living out the ancient truth written about long ago—without a vision for our lives, we perish.

LOST SOUL

*It is an ironic habit of human beings to run faster when
we have lost our way.*

Dr. Rollo May

IN THE SPRING OF 2017, a young man arrived at church wearing beige corduroy pants and a thin hooded sweatshirt—a clear indication that he wasn't a thru-hiker. He looked cold. He stood at six feet, four inches tall. His hair was short, wild, and wavy, full over his forehead and tighter around his ears. It appeared as if he had cut his own hair. Along with his beard, gaunt face, rounded protruding cheekbones, it looked as if his face came to a point at his chin. I could see the outline of his leg bones through his pants as if he had no flesh; a rope held up the waist. The other hikers described him as a "lost soul," yet someone who was harmless. But I wondered if he was harmless to himself?

There was something so gentle and kind about this twenty-something man that even though he wasn't a thru-hiker, we allowed him to stay a few nights. He came to a Sunday morning worship service and sat quietly at the back of the church along with a few other hikers from Germany, Scotland, and Austria. When the service was over, many of us headed over to Fellowship House for coffee hour. Lost Soul was waiting for me.

"I have always had trouble with women in authority, but after today, I no longer do. Christ was at the center of that service," he said.

Since there wasn't much space to talk privately, we agreed to find each other later, or the next day, as I was curious about him. He asked if he could play the piano in the church. I hesitated since our pianist was a bit possessive of the Steinway, and since it was old and a bit fragile, she insisted on coddling the baby grand. I suggested he play the piano at Fellowship House once the coffee hour was underway.

When his dirtied fingers pressed the ivories, it was as if the air caught fire. His notes were clean and pure; harmony and beauty frothed out of the chaos he was. He was writing something, like a letter. We translated what was unwritten into our language, understanding what can never be articulated. It didn't belong to any of us, nor to him who played the old hymns and contemporary Christian music by memory.

The next morning, Lost Soul came into my office smelling of wood and cigarette smoke. He bent his reed-like body onto my couch, but he never stopped moving. It was as if he was always playing the piano, his arms reaching out in front of him, his legs folding and unfolding, feet against invisible pedals, his fingers gesturing as if over mystical keys. He was an arrhythmia of movements and words, his story told in staccato speech. Everything inside me pulled into the tempest he was.

He started at the beginning—how he grew up in a Christian home, had the best father on earth, and a mother who was a backwoods countrywoman from Appalachia. He hadn't been successful in love or life, despite his outrageous talent. He heard voices, he said, and he knew what people were thinking.

"I know I sound crazy," he said often, and the thing was, he did, and he didn't. His sentences and thought processes were a bit frayed but not difficult to follow. He was logical. "People tell me when I tell them what I hear them thinking that I am right."

He grew up attending a conservative evangelical church and won just about every Bible quiz. When someone grows up with an ultraconservative faith as he had, I wondered if such indoctrination can drive a person with an unquiet mind toward lunacy—maybe because frailty and the human condition are enemies of righteousness in some religious understandings.

"After my last fight with my girlfriend during a wedding reception, I went into the woods, and I started beating myself up, screaming, punching, and hitting myself. I took my tie and made it into a noose—I had hit a girl, I hated myself—I tied myself to a tree and I hanged myself, but her family came around me and held me so I couldn't die. The police came, I was arrested, put into a psych ward. I've been on every kind of antipsychotic medication, and I don't want to take them anymore. The only thing that helps is weed, and my parents won't let me come home if I use it. It's the only thing that calms me down."

He told me he couldn't be around people too much. Sleeping in the woods was his best medicine. I imagined the natural world entered him, cooled his fevers, and stilled his singed bones.

That evening, Lost Soul joined Bible study, eager to participate in the discussion as he downed three pieces of homemade banana cake. When the study was over, he made his way to the piano again, and several of us joined him and sang along. But every few minutes, he would jump up, scream out: "I have so much anxiety. I'm too nervous!" It seemed like someone was throwing punches at him from the inside out, something that could not live alongside music. He carried on with our urging, his voice rising to where his spirit could not go. As the strains rose, so shadows shifted over him. Yet his music prayed us to God.

Half an hour later, Lost Soul left us to sleep under a tent of darkness, somewhere off the trail. I imagined him swaddled in a blanket of night, soothed by the wild songs of coyote and fox and raccoon. Did he read the mind of God as he lay there? Were the stars unspoken syllables he deciphered? Was the sky a hieroglyphic?

Before he left the following day, he came to my office and handed me small self-created envelopes made out of notebook paper. He wrote on each—one for the banana cake baker, one for the harmony girls, one for the preacher, and another for David. Inside each one was a four-leaf clover; tradition holds that the fourth leaf of the clover represents good luck; the other three leaves represent faith, hope, and love. I thought that Lost Soul should have carried them with him rather than give them away.

There's a Christian legend about how Eve brought a four-leaf clover with her after being expelled from Paradise. Maybe we all carry a memory of Paradise within ourselves. That memory, more than any-thing else, is what drives us toward discontentment, perhaps even mad-ness, knowing how the world should be, how we should be. Banished from Eden, but never from the remembrance of perfection.

SALVATION TRAIL

You, God, are my God, earnestly I seek you; I thirst for you, my whole being longs for you, in a dry and parched land where there is no water.

Psalm 63:1
New International Version

I WAS FAMILIAR WITH DELAWARE WATER Gap, Pennsylvania, years before it was officially named an AT town and long before I came to serve as pastor of the Church of the Mountain. My oldest daughter, Casey, was living here while commuting to Rutgers University in Newark, New Jersey. In 2005, her sister, Ann, came home after following The Grateful Dead cross-country. Her blonde hair was knotted into dreadlocks; her lime-green eyes were dull; and her clothes baggy, torn, and frayed. Casey led her into the wilderness, up the trail to Mount Minsi to detox, something they hid from me for a long time.

For my loved ones, this wilderness has been a place of deliverance and redemption. On top of Mount Minsi, Ann puked out her poison. From the peak's edge, she could see how far she had fallen from grace. The view of Mount Tammany, the Kittatinny Ridge, the Delaware River, and an endless sky is an ambush of beauty so profound it exorcises demons. I know of nothing more seductive than this affliction of beauty—it lances darkness from the infected heart and anoints the inflicted wound with the balm of air and light. It narrows the gorge between self and God.

There was exodus and exile in Ann's blood. She left at the end of that summer to travel out west to live the life of a young woman who was home nowhere and everywhere at the same time, only to meet a man who had never been home anywhere in his life. Eventually, they came east to settle in the Catskill Mountains, upstate New York, where he originated from. I met Sam when he emerged from a beat-up, paint-weary van, sunblock foil covering every window, and a pit bull locked inside on a warm afternoon. Tall, muscular, with shoulder-length black hair, he had eyes as dark as unpolished onyx; there was no reflection of the world in them. He was fifteen years older than my daughter, had a jailhouse swagger and crude tattoos across his knuckles—something he had to have done to himself with the ink lines uneven and jagged. There was an unholy theater about him.

Being around him was like being in the high desert—the air too thin, the ground parched. It felt that way from the first moment I met him. Worse, it seemed as if he held the title to my daughter's life as if she willingly gave it away. Is this how she understood love? This giving away, this relinquishing of her power, and the awful need for drama? Is this what I had modeled for her?

A year later, Ann called me, her voice buoyant and joyous. She was pregnant; I was going to be a grandmother. I hung up the phone shortly after her announcement. I knew she had wanted a baby; I knew she was infatuated with the romance of being a mother. She didn't know how she would have to ransom her already ransomed life for the child she was carrying.

They lived in a camper on someone else's property; neither had a job that could support a family. In the months that followed, the darkness around Sam grew thornier, more impenetrable, more suffocating, and my fear grew in kind. But the child grew and grew and grew within her. He learned to swim in that inner sea; he swallowed all the songs she sang. They fluttered inside him, like the smallest bird caught in the cage of her ribs.

Albany Medical Center, February 2008
I call . . . early morning
I beg the nurse,
"Please patch me into the room."

I hear you.
Groans and moans
of body stretching until
muscle unravels from bone.

I want to hold you.
I want to gather ice chips,
lay them upon your hot tongue.
I want to tell you how it was for me
giving birth to you,
and how from the earth
of our women's bodies, life comes.
But death comes too,
to who you once were,
to the life you once lived.

Death to an existence once known,
once lived, is forever banished
the moment his seed burrowed in you.
From you grows this tree of life,
with limbs and arms,
with seasons of flourish and drought
with white roots that have reached through centuries.

I cradle the receiver in my hand as if it is you.
I listen to every word, every sigh.
I can't wait for the sound barrier to be broken
by the first shriek of your son.

8:22 I write the time down.
I hear your breathing,
the baby's heartbeat—
they fill the room.
The midwife is counting between pushes.
I gasp. I hold my breath. I push and rest.

My nails dig into my palms.

"You're about to go," she says,
This woman with no name,
mothering my daughter.
I want to be there.
I want to catch her son, our son,
to imprint him with my being,
The mother of his mother.

You cry out.
You're making that transition from childhood
to motherhood; there is no way back.

8:33 You're screaming, "I can't
go through with it." The midwife—
why wife?—tells you, "You're doing great."
She's counting between pushes.
Elementary math . . . within a mystical equation.

8:37 I can't help myself . . .
The rustlings, panicked tears, the counting;
the father tells you that you can do it.
How the hell does he know?
How the hell does any man know?

I can't help but think about the midwives
of the Old Testament . . .
women helping women give birth,
catching sons and daughters in the dark.

The baby's heartbeat is faster,
Amplified. Pauses. Silence. Small conversations.
The baby will enter a world of words.
We wait for his emergence.

8:41 "Push, push, push."
She commands.
You never were very obedient.

8:43 You scream; the earth shatters.
A high-pitched scream. "I'm scared."
"Don't be scared," the midwife says.
But you sob and tremor.

You will never stop that tremor,
my daughter, once he comes.
The world is not hospitable.
You will swallow a tear too many times.
But its salt will make you thirst for God,
when you pray for your son to have a long life.

8:48 They offer you a washcloth.

8:49 "I can't do it." You scream at the walls.
You scream at yourself.
You scream—
you can't endure the pain of it all.

8: 54 "She's doing great, Mom, she's doing really good."
The unnamed woman cheers me.
I hear compassion, gentleness.

9:00 "Put the phone down," you demand the midwife.

9:01 "I can't do it."

9:03 "I can't do it."
Your son's pushing his way into the cold room
into the air and light.

9:06 "I have to cut you, or you'll rip."

She numbs you.
"Take a breath, hold back.
I'm cutting to the side."

9:08 You yelp.
A helpless body-snatching yelp.
"His head is right there."

9:09 Your son falls into the world,
And into his own infant body.

You are sobbing.
"You did it."

I hear the cry.
I am choking as if it is my own first breath.

"Dakotah"
"He's got a full head of hair," she says.

I want to smell him.
I see your face a hundred miles away,
the puzzle in your eyes,
the first time you hold your son—
the bloody glory, exhaustion, pleasure, fear,
the beginning.

DAKOTAH

"Dakotah," a name that means friend in Lakota.

Eight months later, on a hot August afternoon, I hiked up Mount Minsi with my daughters and grandson. We passed Lake Lenape and wandered through trees, dangling vines, and swaying shadows. The air was full of seeds that planted themselves in me, in us. We smelled water nearby and walked toward the sound of a rushing stream. Dakotah, snug in a child's backpack his mother was wearing, kicked his bare feet. On his right ankle was a small scar left by a piece of shattered glass from a framed photograph smashed during one of his father's tirades.

We rested by the stream and let the cool breeze flow over us. I hadn't planned on baptizing Dakotah there but asked if I could, knowing his father would never agree to it in or out of a church. I knew that if I baptized my grandson here, the wilderness would forever be in his blood, as would the mountains and streams.

They reminded me that Ann had asked Casey a few years earlier to baptize her in the Caribbean Sea the day their father remarried. I imagined the warm turquoise water, the lightness of her as Casey held her sister in her arms, the salty sea purifying their drenched bodies. I ached with peace and with sorrow for not bearing witness. I don't know what compelled Ann that day to ask to be baptized or if she thought it would take a sea to wash everything away.

I cupped the chilled water with my hand. Sun glittered in it. I thought of how in every drop of water there is the existence of storm and sea, of river and rain. It holds within it the proof of storms that have come and that will come, of rivers that rush to the sea; a river called time, a sea called humanity. I thought about how rain falls from heaven to water the earth and flows into underground aquifers, believing that faith is that underground aquifer in a person's life. Faith takes all that falls upon it—that seeps into it, and I think that not a drop goes to waste; it wells up within like a spring of living water in times of despair and drought.

"Dakotah, I baptize you in the name of the Father . . ." I poured a handful of water over his head and watched how it dripped down his face, how he caught his breath and looked at me with uncertainty.

I scooped up another handful that trickled down my arm and poured it over his head.

"In the name of the Son . . ." and then with the last handful, ". . . and in the name of the Holy Spirit."

He didn't cry; he furrowed his brows. His eyes, the color of forest—verdant and copper—fastened to me even as he kicked and jumped up and down in the backpack.

"You are claimed for Christ."

We prayed, the three of us, but I don't remember what we said; the sound of the water was enough as it resonated through every cell of his being and of our beings, reminding us that we are a geography of thirst.

Perhaps it was the sounds of water and the names—"Father, Son, and Holy Spirit"—flowing over Dakotah that contained all the sounds and all the words of the universe in every language. Father, Son, and Holy Spirit—the singular dictionary of life. All he had to do was to look up these names for the meaning of his days, for the definition of all that was, all that is, and all that would ever be. In these names, all names.

A HOLE IN THE HEART

The beloved wants to hold us upside down and shake all the nonsense out.

Sufi Mystic, Hafez

E VERYONE IS BORN WITH A hole in their heart that murmurs of deep-down things.

When I was in my late thirties, my physician diagnosed me with a heart murmur, a turbulent rush of blood gushing through valves that he could hear with his stethoscope. Ever since, I've thought the wilderness is a spiritual stethoscope, amplifying what whispers in us. I believe it's that need to hear the deep-down place within that drives mystics to the desert and hikers to the wilderness to self-exile. Sometimes that exile is forced upon us; sometimes, we volunteer for it.

Toiling Midget was determined to finish what her father couldn't years ago when he was sixty-four years old, her age now. She was a spunky, short, spiked-hair woman with a small freckled face accentuated by large turquoise-rimmed glasses. She said her father had set out on the AT the year that it wouldn't stop raining. He was chilled to the bone, soaked through, for nine hundred miles. He had lost so much weight that her mother demanded that he abandon the trail and come home.

"He had a fast metabolism and bad gear," said Toiling Midget, "I am trying to carry on his legacy."

Packing up her gear, she was heading into town for a motel room after having been kept awake by a group of hikers partying the night away, talking up a storm, and drinking beer (despite the signs posted prohibiting alcohol consumption on church grounds). Sometimes respect is hard to find on the trail, as well as at the center. She said an older male hiker was stalking her, camping next to her in the patch of grass between the sanctuary and Fellowship House.

I noticed a swollen yellow pouch below her left eye and asked her about it.

"Oh, well, I slammed head first into a rock fifty miles back or so; bent my glasses all to hell. Love those good ole Pennsylvania rocks. Didn't help that the weight of my pack made my face hit even harder. I had to get my glasses fixed. I'm just glad they didn't break."

Her legs bloomed with different shades of purple, blue, and orange from fading bruises. Several cuts lined her skin, a Morse code of dashes and dots jammed with dried blood. Her bare feet, raw with blisters, looked sore and tender; her toenails were seamed with dirt, and a few of her toes were wrapped with soiled white tape. But at least now she could see her toes; she hadn't been able to see over her girth since she had walked *El Camino* three years earlier. She had shrunk to a more manageable size.

"All this weight I'm carrying made me shorter, I think. Before, I barely stood at four-foot-eleven." We snickered. "I walked the *Camino* and lost fifteen pounds without even trying. I did more than five hundred miles in France to Santiago, then to the Atlantic Ocean, about a thousand miles in about seventy-two days. I traveled during some of that time, had blisters then too, and had to sit around a hotel room for a few days."

I asked her about *El Camino*, otherwise known as the *Pilgrimage de Santiago,* as I had been scheduled to work at the Pilgrim House, a new mission that opened in Santiago before I accepted the position at the Church of the Mountain. I chose to wait until I was immersed in the church before undertaking that short-term mission overseas. Besides, what could be better training than being here at the oldest, continuously-running hikers hostel on the AT? The organization that established the Pilgrim House required that anyone who served there had first to walk *El Camino* for five days, at least; you had to be a pilgrim to minister to one.

The trail is also known as *The Way of Saint James*—named after one of Christ's disciples, who was beheaded around 44 CE and buried in Santiago City. James's body was carried by boat from Jerusalem to northern Spain. Back during the Middle Ages, someone could earn indulgences by walking *The Way* for the forgiveness of sins. But over the centuries, especially starting in the late twentieth century, more and more people came to walk for other reasons.

Toiling Midget had started in Le Puy, France. She explained that a person didn't have to lug all their food, or a tent or sleeping bag, only snacks, clothes, and rain gear. There were many hostels along *the way* that would provide meals and a room to sleep, which might include bunks for sixty as well, stacked three high.

"I should have just carried a silk sleeping bag liner, weighing four ounces. It's hot during the summer, about a hundred degrees. The trail itself is nowhere as difficult as the Appalachian Trail, except in the Pyrenees. At the end of the *Camino*, I took a train from Santiago through the wilds of the country to Madrid; it was spectacular."

She traveled alone but walked a distance with three Irish sisters (biological, not nuns).

"You've got guts," I said.

"I have more guts now than I did when I was younger."

Maybe less to lose, I thought, since aging itself tends to loosen all kinds of things from a person—sight from short distances, tendons from joints and bones, attachments to material possessions. The hole in the heart expands, widens, and everything that once tried to fill it falls out. This is unmistakable grace.

"Most of the people I met weren't walking *El Camino* as a Christian pilgrimage, but they were walking for spiritual reasons. I was Catholic—I didn't do it for that purpose, but the church has a huge role in the *Camino*. It starts in France at a cathedral, where you're sent out with a blessing, and it ends up at a cathedral in Santiago, where St. James's remains are."

She wasn't Catholic or anything now. "Maybe Buddhist, I don't know."

"Were you on a spiritual quest when walking the *Camino*?" I asked.

"It turned into one; it has that effect on people. I saw young Irish cut-ups when they arrived at *Cruz de Ferrer*." She paused. "I'm going to cry now. It was, um, everybody cried, it's been three years, and I still cry. It's incredible. The cross just snuck up on me. I was talking to a Canadian pilgrim about places to visit in the U.S. when we came upon it. There it was, an incredibly emotional experience—it creeps up on everybody. I saw grown men on their knees weeping. It got to me more than the cathedral."

"What was it about that cross?" I asked.

Cruz de Ferrer is a simple, stark iron cross with a pile of stones around it, stones that people bring to leave there with messages or names painted on them.

"Okay, I'm a scientist—pretty much an atheist—but there was something there, something, a presence. I don't know what the source of what it was, some energy. I have felt it in other places, at Ellis Island—millions of souls passed through there; there was trauma there. This was a strange place. These souls came out of the walls at me, and I had to leave. Felt it at the St. Francis of Assisi Church in Italy. I sat in there—my husband felt it too, and he's a total atheist—he had to leave."

A hole in the heart for such *felt presence*. I knew what she spoke of, and I also knew no words could pin down the experience or be sewn to the page or sung into the air. Like God's Hebrew name always written without the vowel: G-d, too holy to pen or speak. An invisible presence through which all else became visible. I thought of TS Eliot's poem, "The Waste Land":

> Who is the third who walks always beside you?
> When I count, there are only you and I together.
> But when I look ahead up the white road
> There is always another one walking beside you.

"So, if you've had those experiences, isn't that worth exploring more?" I probed.

"I believe in Buddhism. I guess agnostic is a better term, I don't know. There are things that we can't see, that we can't test for, that we have no proof one way or another. As a scientist, there is so much we don't understand; that's science—the evidence changes, so you change what you believe."

I let her speak for a while, then I said, "You know, at the times of my greatest doubt, there was always one thing that made me believe. It was my own urge to create that convinced me of a Creator. I would add that there is an innate moral code written into us. And that we search for meaning and purpose. Why do we do that? Can science measure those invisible things?"

She looked down at her feet and wiggled her toes against the soft, cool earth.

"Everything you said is a way of interpreting the world," she said.

"That's true. How do you interpret the world?"

"I have a background in science. I researched stem cells years ago. The things that you think of as miracles are just another way of saying you don't understand what you are seeing. I saw stem cells turn into heart cells, something happens—this isn't new, but at some point, when there are a critical number of cells, and these cells are always talking to each other, they start to beat."

"Beautiful mysteries," I responded.

"Maybe this search for meaning and purpose is what makes us human," she said. "We now know that animals talk to each other; who is to say that cows don't search for meaning? Elephants can separate for their entire lives, and they will recognize one another forty years later. We know now that animals have emotions; they think, they have anger, jealousy, they grieve. They can be devious too; monkeys have proven that."

"Do you think it is possible that all species have a moral code?" I asked.

She didn't answer, but she went on to say, "Buddhism makes me more aware of life and the value of all life."

I taught a college course on comparative religions and remembered how students were attracted to Buddhism as it honors all forms of life and teaches about desire and suffering. Buddhism espouses detachment; all suffering has to do with desire. Unlike Christianity, which teaches us to love one another, care for our neighbor near and far, be attached, and suffer with others.

I asked, "Are you a retired scientist?"

"No. I've done lots of things—art, woodworking, photography—

what I want to do is go back to culinary school and work in an *el barre* in Portugal and feed hikers. Portugal has its pilgrimages that start in Lisbon." She paused, slipping her feet into a pair of Crocs. "I told my husband that this was the time for me to do the trail before it's too late. If I wait, I might not be able to do it. He's not in good shape, and my sister has developed some bizarre ailment. None of us knows how many days we have left before something strikes us down. Do it now —do it while your body still works."

She finished stuffing her gear into the pack, stood to leave, looping one strap over her left shoulder. I saw a scallop shell around her neck, the symbol of the Pilgrimage to Compostela, a physical metaphor for how all pilgrimages lead to the same place—James' tomb in Santiago. Pilgrims are given a scallop shell when they begin their journey. According to one source, the scallop is also a metaphor for God's hand guiding pilgrims to Santiago, just as the waves wash the shells up onto the Galicia's shores. The shell, yellowed from the oils of her skin, struck me as a drinking vessel for water from the shallowest river or stream.

Toiling Midget said goodbye, and I headed toward my office. I thought about the symbol for the AT. So much to see in one simple symbol: mountains, trees, rings of time, branches, roots, a cross, a crown, arms outstretched, head bowed, a universe. Whatever wilderness journey a person undertakes, be it *El Camino* or the AT, I'm convinced there happens a kind of a trembling that shakes all things loose.

I AM, YOU ANXIOUS ONE

I am, you anxious one.
Don't you sense me ready to break
into being at your touch?
My murmurings surround you like shadowy wings.
Can't you see me standing before you
cloaked in stillness?
Hasn't my longing ripened in you
from the beginning
as fruit ripens on the branch?

I am the dream you are dreaming.
When you want to awaken, I am that wanting:
I grow strong in the beauty you behold.
And with the silence of stars I enfold
your cities made by time.

R.M. Rilke

LOVE IN THE TIME
OF CORONA

The only regret I will have in dying is if it is not for love.

Gabriel García Márquez

I WAS WORKING ON WRITING AN upcoming wedding ceremony for a woman who once worked at the Travel Center of America truck stop, commonly known as the "TA," in nearby Columbia, New Jersey, where I've served as a chaplain for fourteen years.

I was to meet her later that day on the AT, with a sufficient amount of physical distancing, when it occurred to me that the letters TA and AT were the same, only reversed. Maybe this is what happens when you have been self-quarantining for nearly a month that these epiphanies come to you. Sophia had worked at the truck stop for years until the day she partially mooned a customer, something not out of her sphere of impulsive humor.

Nothing was going to stop this wedding, not even the pandemic of 2020. It was April Fool's Day or nothing, she said. It was our first communication since she left the truck stop nearly five years earlier. I agreed, as long as we respected the mandate for physical distance, I told her.

She and her fiancé had a daughter, Chloe, twenty-five years ago, who had blessed them with two granddaughters. They were determined to surprise Chloe as she walked down the trail to Lake Lenape, where I had officiated another wedding years earlier. Chloe would be lugging her five-month-old baby in a carrier, while the grandfather, the groom, would be clutching her three-year-old's hand on this gray, barely warm day, thinking they were going for a short hike together.

I arrived a little after two in the afternoon, wearing jeans, knee-high black boots, a heavy turtleneck, and a long sweater coat over it, as it was chilly and windy. The parking lot of the trailhead was packed. People milled around too close to one another as if the forest air—spiced with spruce and pine—would protect them from COVID-19. With no space to park, I drove down the road, and walked up the rather steep incline, stopping every so often to catch my breath.

Sophia waited at the closed gate to the trail. She carried a white garment bag with the wedding dress she had bought twenty-nine years ago but never wore. She wore leggings, sneakers, and a sweatshirt. Her long dark hair, parted in the middle, cascaded over her shoulders and chest. She wore little or no makeup, from what I could see. One thing I had remembered about Sophia is that laughter was her language that made her sentences float. She was hard not to like.

Her other daughter, eighteen-year-old Kathy, waited alongside her, wearing skull leggings and a black sweatshirt. Most distinguishing though was her thick, wavy brunette hair like two dark curtains on the stage of her face.

We made our way up the trail and to Lake Lenape, where Sophia unzipped the garment bag and placed it on the picnic table there. She pulled out the long shiny white wedding dress, complete with a six-foot train.

"I tried it on the other day. I could get it up over my hips, but I couldn't zip it up by myself," she said, as she tore off her sweatshirt, revealing a tank top beneath, and began inching the dress up from her feet. It fit up to her waist. She pulled each sleeve up over her arms, but there was no zipping the back shut. The back of the dress flopped at her sides like wings.

I suggested Sophia remove the laces from her sneakers and weave them across the back of the dress and through a hole in the tulle that edged each shoulder of the sleeves, then tie them together to hold the back of the dress from slipping off. We laughed at the predicament, but the ill-fitting wedding dress, the sneakers, all seemed right for an April Fool's wedding in the midst of the pandemic. The lace web sort of worked. Next, the veil was draped and pinned to the crown of her head, reminding me of the flying nun's headpiece. It hid her open back.

All of this while keeping physical distance. The fifty-six-year-old bride, wearing laceless gray Keds, worked her way to a boulder for photos.

"Mom, you look like the Bride of Chucky," her daughter said, snapping away on her phone's camera.

By now, it was close to three o'clock. Sophia had called her groom, Ron, who was on his way with their daughter and granddaughters. As we waited, the sun came out for a brief moment, lighting up the darkened sky and outlining clouds that looked like angels flocking. I shed my sweater coat and tilted my face up toward the sun and bathed in the warmth.

I offered to take photographs of the bride and daughter, both sprawled out on the boulder. Hikers passed by, curious and engaging in brief conversations, asking if a wedding was happening or if we were doing a film? We waited, Kathy with her cellphone in hand, perched for recording as Ron and Chloe walked down the trail, children in tow, in an attempt to capture the surprise on Ron's face for seeing his bride in a wedding dress. To capture Chloe's face too as they wanted to surprise her with her parents finally going to tie the knot since their lives had been tangled together for decades.

As they rounded the bend and approached, Ron said that someone in the parking lot had asked if they were here for the wedding. Chloe still didn't realize the set-up. The older granddaughter ran ahead and jumped into Kathy's arms and then made a beeline for the lake.

When Ron saw his bride in her gown, with the open back, he said: "You are one class act," and he laughed. Ron, a slight man with a smoker's cough, was a few years older than Sophia. He wore khaki pants and a black fleece jacket and complained it was too cold and windy.

As the ceremony began, they stood six feet away from me, but they could not stand still as the three-year-old demanded to be held. Ron had sunglasses on, and a cigarette hanging from his lips that he finally crushed underfoot as I began.

"Today, we are gathered here to celebrate love in the time of Corona, even as we practice social distancing. We come together to join two people in holy matrimony, who have taken a long time to get here.

I celebrate you both and your decision to commit yourselves to one another on April Fool's Day. Love makes fools of us all—fools in the sense that we know there is nothing better or more powerful than love and its fearless commitment to be there for one another, come what may in the future."

I shared a brief statement about marriage, how it is God-given for help and comfort. I prayed, even as Sophia and Ron continued to wrestle with their granddaughter. Chloe flanked them to the right, and Kathy videotaped the ceremony, standing several feet away to my right.

I read one of my favorite passages from the Old Testament—how two are better than one, for when one falls, someone is there to pick them up, and when it is cold, there is someone to keep them warm. Every time I read that passage, I think of how practical and humanizing marriage is.

"Sophia and Ron, you met each other in 1992, and as Sophia shared with me, it wasn't exactly love at first sight. The faster you chased her, the faster she ran. Then when Sophia stopped running, you, Ron, started running. The love was always there—just not the timing. You both have had other relationships, but you always came back to each other (at least eight times). Finally, one daughter and two granddaughters later, you decided to stop and give this a real shot. Sophia says it's because you are too old to run now."

I found myself skipping through some of what I had written for the sake of time as they wrestled to keep the three-year-old from diving into the frigid water. Before they said their vows, I asked Ron to take off his sunglasses. Vows said, rings slipped on each other's fingers, I pronounced them husband and wife, said a blessing and a prayer, and invited Ron to kiss his bride, as the veil flew up and over them like a holy spirit.

Love during the time of Corona had won out. Several days later, Sophia texted me about obtaining an official copy of the marriage certificate, now that the courthouse was under lockdown. I asked her how married life was. She responded: "Thanks for the best day of my life. I have loved him forever."

A FATHER'S LETTER

The proper definition of a man is an animal that writes letters.

Lewis Carroll

I picked up a piece of paper folded into eighths off the ground outside my office. It looked like it had fallen out of a hiker's backpack. I unfolded it, saw that it was a letter and that the paper was torn from a black and white composition book with the threaded binding; its edge all jagged. It was signed "Dad" and written so that the torn edge was to the right.

> *Fran,*
>
> *I miss you and love you so very, very much. I have written so many letters and emails to you in the last couple of years, but I never sent them. I was not sure you wanted them, and I did not want to cause you trouble.*
>
> *Charlie tells me how great you are doing. I am not surprised. You are one of the strongest and bravest people I know. I understand you are married now and are going to have a baby. You are going to be an amazing mom. It is good you have someone you trust and love to help you.*
>
> *But this note is not about anyone else. It is about you*

and me. I don't know why you said the things you said. I guess I don't really care why. Being a father to you and your sister was my favorite thing. It was my only thing. I can't believe you are not in my life.

What you decide to do with this letter is up to you. What happens next is up to you. I am not going anywhere. I have always and will always be here.

I dream every single day about getting to see you, hug you, talk to you. I love you more than you can ever know, and I am proud of you.

Dad

He'd have to write another letter, I thought as I held it in my hand. I tried to imagine what had happened between them, what happens between fathers and daughters, mothers and sons, sisters and brothers, and why loved ones withhold forgiveness. I wondered if he was hiking the AT to work through whatever had separated them, every step like a sledgehammer breaking down the wall of silence between them.

A few days later, on a sweltering July afternoon, Pastor Ned came from Asbury Park, New Jersey, along with his wife and son, to investigate the Hikers Ministry, see the Hikers Center, witness the Thursday evening potluck dinner, and speak with hikers. He was contemplating opening up hiker hostels in all fourteen states along the AT as a ministry. His wife, Sarah, had long auburn hair with gray roots and hazel eyes; she stood by her man in quiet repose. Their tall and splintery sixteen-year-old son was clean-cut. As I walked with them, I noticed he was also silent, as if he had no voice.

"I'm an evangelist," Ned said, "that's my gift." He had a shaved head and a long, narrow beard that reminded me of a horse's tail. Burly is the best word to describe his stature. But there was something in his eyes, something hard and sharp, bullet-like as if he had seen things he should never have seen and could never stop seeing. "I grew up with

Satanists and pagans. I worked as a thug for the mob, and I was a drug addict before I came to Christ. My church is filled with people like me, people with a past, people nobody else wants in their churches. I've Hell's Angels in my church, guys who have committed heinous crimes. I just love 'em into the Kingdom."

He was tattoo-ridden, with skulls and crosses and evil-looking angels inked all over his arms and neck. I couldn't tell where else the dark images may have imprinted his body since most of his skin was covered by a short sleeve t-shirt and jeans. They showed a story I didn't want to read. Fancy letters were inked on each of his knuckles, but I couldn't decipher what the words or initials were, as his hands were never still. I didn't get a chance to ask about them.

He and Sarah had married long before coming to faith, he told me. It wasn't difficult to imagine both of them riding in a motorcycle gang when they were younger; they looked to be in their mid to late forties now. He explained that he was being ordained with the Christian and Missionary Alliance Church and was finishing up his studies even though he had already been pastoring a church for the last few years. I feared he'd dominate the dinner with an altar call, knowing hikers had already been exposed to aggressive evangelism on the trail.

"We don't preach to our hikers," I said. "We don't corner them during dinner; we ask them about their lives, their stories, and experiences on the trail. I've learned as a pastor and as a truck stop chaplain that if you listen long and hard enough to anyone, eventually just about every conversation comes around to God all on its own because God's in our DNA, there's no escaping God. It never has to be forced or maneuvered." I waited for him to correct me.

He repeated, "I love 'em to Christ. I can talk to anyone about Jesus."

His wife was attentive and quiet, slanting her body toward her husband as if admiring him. She and I exchanged occasional glances. Their son stared out into the trees around the back porch as if the trees were the only elders to listen to; his body angled slightly away from us. For a moment, it felt to me as though Ned was there by himself.

A team of women and men started to prepare for the meal, so I excused myself and helped set up the tables, wipe them down, cover a few with fresh white paper where the food would be placed. I chatted with the grill master, Bill, as the sizzle and scent of hot dogs wafted through the air. "These are gourmet hot dogs, fifty-percent fat and fifty-percent salt," he said, then laughed at his quip.

Larry had set up the homemade ice cream machine that began churning cream and sugar and fresh cherries. We set out the plates, napkins, plastic utensils, and salt and pepper shakers. We then placed ketchup and mustard on each of the six long tables. A few hikers came early and helped by sweeping the porch and aligning plastic garbage bags in the trash cans. Ned talked to one of them, a young man, but I couldn't hear the conversation.

I didn't sit with Ned or his family during the potluck dinner so that he could engage with the hikers and ask them what he wanted to know. I sat with two thru-hikers from Canada, a husband and wife who had recently retired. The husband had been a police officer and a police chaplain, and the wife had been a nurse.

"I had to stop being a chaplain," he said, with a Canadian lilt to his voice. "I burned out, couldn't deal with the sadness of it, all the funerals."

I thought about the weight of sorrow and that father's letter—about the malignancy of abandonment, whether through choice, an emotional crime or death, or some other force; how that weight can compress and sometimes crush the humanity in us all.

Toward the end of the meal, I moved to the table where Ned and his family sat. We continued talking about how the Christian and Missionary Alliance Church trained and educated its ministers.

Ned started in: "Part of my ministry training involved going to a conference where the leader spoke of unforgiveness as a chain that binds us, as a way the devil gets in, gets a foothold. I was delivered that night. I woke up from a dream, and I literally felt and heard this presence leave me with a whooshing sound. I asked a friend of mine the next day if he'd been praying for me that night, and he said a team of men had been."

I wanted to ask if he had suffered from unforgiveness, either his own or others', knowing there was much of his story that he hadn't shared, like the decades when he was working for a major crime family in New Jersey. He said he felt free of a spirit he didn't even know lived inside him. I nodded as he spoke as if agreeing with what he said, even though I wasn't sure what I had come to believe about "demon possession" over the years.

I said: "I saw a friend of mine undergo what they said was an exorcism once, a long time ago at a Kathryn Kuhlman service in the early 1970s. I knew Trevor was troubled. A group of men surrounded him and prayed for him at his request, and then I saw him writhing on the floor. They yelled out, 'What is your name,' and Trevor answered, 'Incest.' Never forget that, but I've never seen anything like it since."

"The pastor who led the weeklong seminar on Soul Care said it starts with unforgiveness—it's the chain that binds us," Ned repeated.

I imagined the rushing sound of a demonic spirit fleeing a body; did that demon go by a human's name, someone Ned hadn't forgiven or who hadn't forgiven him?

What about the daughter who seemingly couldn't forgive her father, evident in the letter I had found only a few days earlier? Couldn't or wouldn't forgive? Did she feel that shackle around her, holding her down, holding her back? Might it be the same chain that would one day strangle the relationship she could have had with her son or daughter? Maybe unforgiveness is passed down, generation to generation, I thought, as I sent Ned and his invisible family on their way a while later to investigate the town and walk over to the trailhead.

By now, some of the hikers were hanging out by the smoking table, toking away on hand-rolled cigarettes. Others were preparing to bed down for the night, pitching their tents between the Fellowship House and the sanctuary even though it wasn't dark yet. Another group gathered around the table outside the center. I took some leftover food to them to chow down on later, warning them not to leave any food outside for the bears.

"Thank you so much," one hiker after another said. "Thank you for the feed, for putting us up, for these great accommodations. Best shower on the trail."

Voices faded as I walked toward my truck, but there was anything but the quiet of nightfall in me. I felt disturbed, unsure if Ned was right to be so aggressive and bold. Or was I held captive by fear or past experiences of evangelists who sentenced others to damnation with such self-righteousness? Ned wasn't one of them; he had witnessed hell; it had burned inside him once; there were flames imprinted on his skin, tattooed in ash-colored ink. Memories of being godless had scarred him, terrified him still, it seemed. He had spoken of redemption and resurrection, but it was the things he left unspoken that left me haunted, things that hovered in silence. Ned's story was his power, his proof of salvation and God, his proof of life. I knew that was why he could speak of nothing else. He was a living document, and his story, like all stories, is in its own right a sacrament.

ADOPTED

The bond that links your true family is not one of blood,
but of respect and joy in each other's life.

Richard Bach

FOR FIVE WEEKS IN JULY and August of 2018, it rained hard almost every day, flooding the Delaware River, submerging docks and boulders and islands, and eroding the good earth. Hikers spoke of trees falling across the trail as the ground was so saturated, roots could no longer hold the weight they bore. The rain drove the last of the Springer Mountain crowd into the center. They would have to make up for lost time, as it was getting almost too late to make it to Maine before Baxter State Park would close. Long-distance hiking made room for an unstable and unpredictable life, for dodging limbs, for having to pay attention to the weather and its dangers, including slippery ground and slick rocks. A few hikers hobbled in with twisted ankles, broken toes, and sprained knees.

Soaked packs hung from branches, tents were folded over every railing possible throughout the church grounds, clothes were draped on racks, but the air was too heavy, and everything remained soggy and stinky. Inside the center, the smell of wet socks contaminated the atmosphere even as fans blew on them. Mildew, like a splatter of dark rain, stained packs, gear, and clothing, tinging the air with its musk. Clods of mud left a trace both inside and outside the center.

Hikers were restless, anxious to move again, fearing if they stalled for too long, it would force them to abandon their hike and, I suspected, that they couldn't get their internal engines going again and would be tempted to quit. Either way, they were grateful for four sturdy walls, a hot shower, and light to read and write by. One day, a hiker was way-laid after her pup got bit by a copperhead. Luckily, she had been able to find a vet, but she was going off the trail for a week so that her dog could recover and rebuild his strength. Her father was driving in from Michigan to pick them up.

The rain itself mirrored the world wherein it fell and seemed to encourage contemplation, reflection, and solitude that made the hikers withdraw from each other. I have often wondered if hiking the trail in and of itself was a way to prove something either to oneself or to the world; if it's a way to become visible to the world that left too many feeling that they were invisible.

It had been a week since I had found the letter written from a fa-ther to a daughter when I came across two sheets of what I thought was an autobiography. The pages were written in pencil, printed, and each page claimed the same last name but different first names. On one page, the name was Sasha Gire:

I was born on May 14, 2001. I am adopted from Ukraine by John and Donna Gire, who got me when I was twelve years old. They wanted to homeschool me, but that didn't work out, so they put me in public school (Hickory Middle School). I spend three years in that school and wrestled for two of those years. When I turned fifteen, I was homeschooled again because I was behind in school. After I turned sixteen, I attended to Commonwealth Challenge Program. I had a hard time in life. It's a Military School.

I learned that people only get one chance in their life because second and third chances are very rare. It's all from God, who loved me and never gave up on me. Even when I did, he was still calling my name; that's when I got adopted. I'm planning to go into the Marines as my job for twenty years, then open a mechanic shop as my regular job, and if none of these things work out, I have an uncle who will give me a job. If I didn't like that job, then I would go to Bible College and become a pastor to travel around the world and spread the gospel about Christ.

A square from the lower right corner of the page had been torn off, and there were about six lines left empty. The other page read:

My name is Tigran John Gire. I got my middle name John because I'm awfully good-looking. Now I wasn't always alluringly gratifyingly gorgeous, that came later, but my story starts in the place far, far away. I was born four weeks early in the place that most people can't even comprehend, even in their worst nightmares. Both of my biological parents died before I could speak.

Consequently, when I was around three years old, I was sent to orphanage. Nine dire years have passed from there, with events too gruesome to write on this page. When I was eleven years old when my first unbelievable miracle happened, an event that absolutely rocked my dreadful world. I was adopted by a lovely couple; that was the birth of my new life, a beginning of a new story. There were no words to describe how I felt at that time.

Over the six years of living in America, I traveled around by going to different states and different countries. I did wrestling for quite a while, becoming a beast in what I did simply because I refused to give up, so when I fell, I got up again. When I was sixteen years old, I ran my first marathon. Now I am seventeen and on my way to finishing the Appalachian Trail, which is 2,200 miles. My future goal is to become U.S. Navy Seal so I can help protect this country and my family.

I was not sure upon reading the pages if they were a part of some fictional work or memoir. Similarities and differences in the narratives were apparent—an internationally adopted orphan who makes good in America and grows up to serve in the armed services, whatever branch he decided on. Maybe identity is more fluid than any of us think. However, writing it all down may have been his deliberate and conscious way of staking his claim on life itself and his right to exist. Somehow, words create inhabitable, self-contained worlds. I wondered if perhaps they were brothers hiking the trail together.

Reading about being in an orphanage in Ukraine brought me back to a series of articles I had written years earlier about international adoption. After their publication, a couple had called to tell me that they were on the way to adopt a son and daughter from an orphanage in Russia; how they had given up hope of having a family before reading the articles. The soon-to-be-mom shared with me the conditions they had witnessed upon their first trip to Russia months earlier—of the shortage of caregivers, the urine-soaked crib sheets, the blankets placed over the radiators to dry that made the rooms smell of human ammonia. Most frightful, though, were the children behind the bars of their cribs left to themselves most hours of the day. Another sad truth was that many children's parents were not dead but had been lost to alcoholism.

There are no orphans on the trail. Hikers adopt one another, at least for a time, calling each other family as they look out for one another. On occasion, they form human chains to help one another up a scramble or cross a rushing stream. They check in at shelters and hostels to see where their hiking buddies are or wait for them to return; sometimes, they help carry another's gear to make the load lighter if one is injured. Hiking buddies often become lifelong friends, and they make plans to walk a section of the AT or some other trail together in the years ahead.

Known only by their trail names, with no birth names, perhaps they bond more naturally. But even more so, the wilderness itself becomes home. And eventually, if they walk far and deep enough into the woods, into the rain, into the beauty, they understand they first and foremost belong to the earth, to the trees and rivers and lakes and rocks and cliffs, and that they are made of clay and rain, roots and wind, sky and sun.

ALL THAT REMAINS

My room is so quiet and empty it hurts.

Nina LaCour

A NAVY MAN FOUND HER DEAD two years after she was reported missing. All that remained of Geraldine A. Largay was found in a sleeping bag inside her tent on the top of a mountain in Maine. She had been waiting to be rescued before she waited for death to come. The game wardens knew it was her. Her identification papers were all there, along with her journal.

I don't know if she passed through Delaware Water Gap or stayed at the Hikers Center on her thru-hike in 2013. It was the year before I was called to serve here. Who would have remembered her? She would have been one in over a thousand in 2013, one of a few women in their sixties with an acute sense that life was passing by quicker now, and it was now or never to do this one thing.

From newspaper photographs, she had close-set eyes and a narrow bridge for a nose; she wore eyeglasses, gold hoop earrings, and a cotton brimmed hat. A man's hand, with a gold wedding band, is seen resting on her left shoulder. Her teeth look perfect, visible in a wide smile.

If faces tell a story of days and how one's days are spent—in privilege or poverty, in sobriety or drunkenness, addiction or admiration—hers looked as if she came from privilege; life had been kind to her. I wondered what changed in her final days, all alone.

I imagined she cried hard, knowing she wouldn't be found in time, even as she knew her husband would be searching for her when she didn't show up at their rendezvous point.

She wasn't far from the AT or the Carrabassett River that could have sustained her. How could the search party miss her, so close to where she had wandered off? I wondered if she could hear the river rushing in the distance. Maybe it was fear that killed her, that paralyzed her. Maybe it was just her time, some people said. What was it like to wait for death to come?

She kept a journal for her husband and daughter and locked it away in a waterproof bag. Words left behind but spoken forever.

What would anyone's last words be, knowing they were dying, alone, in the wilderness? I imagined loneliness hollowed out her bones long before death would come. Ounce by ounce, hopelessness emptied her until she could bear it no longer.

Reading the news article about her remains—I prayed the trees sang to her during her final moments as she lay hungry and thirsty. I prayed they reached out to cover her and to carry her spirit home.

When she fell asleep at last, I believe she dreamt of her husband's voice shouting out to her and her daughter's arms around her.

"When you find my body, please call my husband George and my daughter Kerry," she wrote. "It will be the greatest kindness for them to know that I am dead and where you found me — no matter how many years from now."[2]

She was afraid of being alone, deathly afraid, *The New York Times* reported; she had a history of anxiety and panic attacks.

They looked for her over the next twenty-six months; found her remains less than a mile from the trail. Game wardens carried her out in a white plastic bag—she didn't weigh much, one could tell, by the way they carried her.

Some people say it is morbid to speak of death and one's passing. Others, like me, believe it is essential to consider what will remain after we are gone and if we lived lives worth living. Did we honor

---

2   Bidgood, Jess, and Richard Pérez-peña. "Geraldine Largay's Wrong Turn: Death on the Appalachian Trail." *The New York Times*. The New York Times, May 26, 2016. https://www.nytimes.com/2016/05/27/us/missing-hiker-geraldine-largay-appalachian-trail-maine.html.

it with a fair amount of risk? Did we seek until we found what truly satisfies? Did we try desperately to find our way back once we knew we were lost, or did we wait to be found?

Hikers say they want to lose themselves on the trail without getting lost, something that's easy to do if they step off the path. Everyone should have someone who watches out for them, stands guard, and calls them back if they step too far into the woods.

VIOLENCE

*Have regard for your covenant, because haunts of
violence fill the dark places of the land.*

Psalm 74:20
New International Version

A LTHOUGH THE HIKERS CENTER AT the Church of the Mountain provides sanctuary, it hasn't been exempt from violence. In 1996, twenty years after the center was established, hiker Edward Driggers and fellow hiker and friend, Richard Sealy, had come off the AT and were bunking down for the night when Lawrence Doughty stumbled into the hostel intoxicated, belligerent, and violent. According to police reports, this was what transpired:

"I ought to kill you punks," Doughty said, then pulled out a buck knife and waved it at Driggers. Sealy was lying down on one of the upper bunks.

Then Doughty grabbed a shovel and swung it, just missing Sealy's head. He started to swing it again when Driggers retrieved a.32 caliber revolver from his backpack and told Doughty to step back. Doughty ignored him.

Driggers fired a warning shot, but Doughty didn't back away. In the act of self-defense, Driggers shot Doughty in the chest.

It turns out that Doughty had been staying at the center for several weeks and was working at a nearby university as a dishwasher. From that time on, the Church enforced a policy of a two-night stay at the center, and it was for thru-hikers or section-hikers only, no exceptions. Driggers was not charged with any crime since his action was deemed self-defense. To the church's credit, this violent act did not deter their ministry.

* * *

During my first summer at the church in 2014, a fight broke out in the center between two men. It was mid-August when a homeless young man came to stay, dressed in black, a wide-brimmed hat pulled down over his eyes. He drank openly, despite signs posted everywhere that alcohol is prohibited on the grounds. He said he was looking for a couple of friends, one a local bartender, the other a cokehead. A hiker told him he had to leave. No one confessed to throwing the first punch, but a fight broke out. The police were called; the intruder was carted off in handcuffs.

In May 2019, a man known as Sovereign on the trail, who had threatened to set a tent on fire and burn four hikers to death, killed a man with his 17-inch survival knife and seriously injured a woman. The man who was murdered was forty-three-year-old Ronald S. Sanchez Jr., of Oklahoma, trail name Stronghold, who served three tours in Iraq and Afghanistan and took up hiking to manage his post-traumatic stress disorder.

According to a number of news reports, Sovereign had made a series of terroristic threats for days and weeks before the killing and was arrested. However, the hikers who witnessed his threats did not want to get off the trail to testify, so he was released, carrying out his threat within days in Virginia.

A month later, Stronghold's girlfriend called me, asking if she could send a resupply box to the church for the hikers that contained olive oil packets, energy bars, and other nonperishable foods. It arrived with a brief note: "Here are some of Ron 'Stronghold' Sanchez's supplies. I hope some hikers can use them! Thanks for passing them on. Brenda"

During the following Thursday potluck dinner, we shared Stronghold's story and how the box was given in his memory and honor. Opening the box was like opening a wound. Sorrow bled out, invisible but palpable, and it was as if no one wanted to reach in and touch the supplies, as if they should have been buried with *Stronghold,* knowing that only weeks earlier, he had organized and packed all the things he would need to survive the trail.

There have been many other crimes that have happened along the trail. Federal agents arrested James Hammes, a fugitive who had been on the run for six years, hiding out on the AT under the trail name Bismarck. Psychologists speculated that James needed to belong to some community; it is, after all, a human requirement to be a part of something larger than oneself, even if one is on the lam. He is alleged to have embezzled millions of dollars from his employer, Pepsi. Later it was reported that he was also being investigated for the murder of his first wife, killed in a house fire twelve years earlier.

The Appalachian Trail Conservancy reports that there have been nine homicide victims in seven cases in the history of the AT that has a population of two to three million visitors per year prior to 2019.

On August 12, 2011, the body of long-distance hiker Scott "Stonewall" Lilly, 30, of South Bend, Indiana, was found by other hikers along a side trail between the AT and a shelter in northwest Amherst County, Virginia. Lilly had been hiking alone from southern Pennsylvania toward the trail's southern end on Springer Mountain, Georgia. A state medical examiner later ruled the death a homicide, with the cause of death given as "asphyxia by suffocation." The investigation continues.

January 1, 2008: Meredith Emerson, 24, of Buford, Georgia, went for a day hike on Blood Mountain with her dog and was abducted after a fight from a side trail near a parking lot by drifter Gary M. Hilton. He took her to various ATMs in the area and killed her with a shovel blow to the head south of Amicalola Falls State Park at the end of the week. He was captured soon afterward and negotiated a life sentence plea deal quickly. He was later convicted of the other homicides and is currently on death row in Florida.

September 12, 1990: Thru-hikers Molly LaRue, 25, of Shaker Heights, Ohio, and boyfriend Geoffrey Hood, 26, of Signal Mountain, Tennessee, were killed (throat slit and shot, respectively) as they woke up at a shelter on the trail south of Duncannon, Pennsylvania, by fugitive and drifter P. David Crews, who was arrested walking on the trail into Harpers Ferry eight days later. Crews was sentenced to death in May 1991 in Pennsylvania, but in 2006, Justice Samuel Alito (then an appellate judge in Philadelphia) vacated the sentence on technical grounds. Perry County later agreed to a life sentence to avoid retrial expenses.

May 1988: Hikers Rebecca Wight of Blacksburg, Virginia, 29, and Claudia Brenner, 31, of Ithaca, New York, were accosted near a shelter in Michaux State Forest in south-central Pennsylvania by Stephen Roy Carr, a fugitive who literally lived under a rock in the forest. Carr later stalked them when they moved their campsite to a spot off a side trail and shot at them eight times with a rifle from the woods. Wight died at the scene, but Brenner, with several wounds, escaped and ran through the night to authorities. Carr was arrested at a church about ten days later and eventually sentenced to life in prison.

May 1981: Thru-hiker Robert Mountford, 27, and coworker Susan Ramsey, 27, who had just joined him for a short time, both of Ellsworth, Maine, were killed during the night near a shelter in southwest Virginia about twenty miles south of Pearisburg. He was shot at the shelter, and she was stabbed to death a short distance away. Both bodies were partially buried but discovered within days. Randall Lee Smith was arrested a few weeks later in Myrtle Beach, South Carolina, and convicted of the crimes, although some evidence had been compromised and the gun was never recovered. He served a full term on reduced charges and was released in September 1996 under strong home-detention parole for ten years. His home abutted the trail south of Pearisburg.

April 1975: Northbound thru-hiker Janice Balza, 22, of Madison, Wisconsin, was killed by a hatchet wielding southbound thru-hiker, Paul Bigley, 51, after breakfast at a shelter in northeast Tennessee. He coveted her pack, testimony at trial revealed. He died in state prison in Nashville.

May 1974: Joel Polsom, 26, of Hartsville, South Carolina, thought to be a thru-hiker, was killed at a Georgia shelter by Michigan fugitive Ralph Fox, who continued to walk south with Fox's girlfriend in tow and later caught a bus to Atlanta, where he was arrested.

The AT, once a warpath, sometimes still is.

CHEROKEE

In the middle of the journey of our life I came to myself within a dark wood where the straight way was lost.

Dante Alighieri

CHEROKEE TRUDGED UP THE CHURCH driveway in late November, alone. His lopsided eyeglass frames were held together by dingy white tape, his jacket torn, along with the dark jeans he wore. His left cheek had a bruise that had faded to an orangish-yellow. He carried nothing, said he had lost his gear after a twenty-foot fall off a cliff while hiking, not far back. He looked beat-up and weary. His clothes smelled of woodsmoke. Said he had lost his wallet, cash, and identification papers, too, on that spill. He was lucky to survive. As a twenty-something-year-old, youth had been on his side.

It was almost Thanksgiving, and although it was a mild November, we knew he couldn't survive without proper gear. He wanted to go home; his body was too broken, he said, and he was too defeated to continue hiking. Home was down south in Kentucky. Could the church help him get there?

One aspect of ministry is that you never know who is telling you the truth and who is trying to scam the church. It happens all the time—someone calls the office looking for assistance and expects help to buy food, pay an electric bill, and put gas in their car, even though they have no relationship with the church. There's always a sad story, and typically, it's the same people repeatedly.

Cherokee called home to inform his parents and asked for financial help, but he couldn't pick up any wired money without identification. He seemed highly anxious; his hands trembled when he talked.

David and I decided to use some of the pastor's discretionary fund to purchase a bus ticket for Cherokee and give him some cash for meals since the journey would take over twenty-four hours. Like everyone the church helps, he promised to pay us back the several hundreds of dollars we gave him; like all, the funds were never reimbursed.

He left the following morning before I arrived at the office, having walked the short distance down Main Street to the bus depot. When I went inside the Hikers Center, I found the following poem he had written:

From Cherokee to the Church

Today with the help from the church a bus ticket bought, I depart,
You'll never know how much you've touched my heart.

This morning on the bus headed home on my way,
Just in time for Thanksgiving Day.

My journey on the trail is a little bitter sweet,
GOD's Church & people here was so glad to meet,

When I fell both sad & with some fear,
The A.T. I can attempt again some other year

My decision to get off trail was a big defeat,
But had a chance to meet cool people hiking in some heat.

I am so grateful for all that you do,
May the spirit of GOD be continuing with you

Given a little money so I could eat
Your gracious help maybe enough meet & greet.

May your Church be humble enough to kneel,
My broken up body needs time to heal.

Raise your hands in prayer to GOD
Fear not ~~moses~~ rod

Thanks again for all you do.
See you again soon with a plan anew.

Josh,
Cherokee

END OF THE TRAIL

When we tire of well-worn ways, we seek for new. This restless craving in the souls of men spurs them to climb, and to seek the mountain view.

Ella Wheeler Wilcox

ASH WEDNESDAY, 2016

I had reached out to ISO months earlier, inquiring about his welfare: "With the trail completed, I wonder how you are, where you are?"

It was early February, and I was working on an Ash Wednesday Service. "Death calls us to life. It reminds us there is a beginning and an end, that this life is but a passing vapor," I wrote. "My mother and I spoke a while ago about the difficulties of aging, about the constant state of mourning the elderly find themselves in: spouses die, sometimes children pass before they do; health declines, eyesight fades, hearing diminishes; independence is threatened. As we spoke, I shared with her what I have come to believe about aging—that it's God's way of helping us let go of our grip of this wonderful thing we call life. No matter how difficult, no matter how many sorrows we have had, no matter how many losses, there are so many more gains; there are so many moments of sheer wonder and awe, so much beauty. Who would leave it willingly?"

I was curious, had ISO found peace, had he been able to let go of the grief that had consumed him?

"Ashes to ashes, dust to dust. From dust, we are created, and to dust, we shall return. In the beginning, God gathered the dust and breathed His life into us . . . and we were born. The wind of God is in us, and it is a mighty wind. It stirs us to love, move in the world, be on fire, and be light," I pressed on.

Strangely enough, at the writing of the last word "light," an email came from ISO. With it, a black and white photograph of him bowing on the ladder on top of Mt. Katahdin, taken late August 2015. There was a reverence to the image; he wasn't looking out at the clouds that were below him, but it appeared as if he was looking inside himself.

I continued to work on the service even as I stared at the photograph. "In the ashes, in their darkness, in the smell of fire they contain, may the hope of the One who is beyond us, who designed, and created all that is, who is as present as the air we breathe, dwell within us."

Those who would gather tonight for the service would come forward with this bidding. Their bodies would groan as they edged off the wooden pews, and the pews would moan as they were held onto for support, slightly loosened from the ancient screws that bolted them to the floor. The people's gentle and hushed footsteps on the carpet would sound like the lapping of a slow-moving tide.

I would mark each person's forehead with the mix of palm ashes and olive oil; the crosses would shimmer in the sanctuary's dim candlelight that evening as it had the year before. Anointing their foreheads with the dark mix, I would say: "Before you return to your seat, pick up one nail from the table behind me and place it where you pray, where you will see it every day. Bring it back on Good Friday and leave it at the cross.

"Reflect on how the nails were used to nail Jesus on the cross, how they were weapons of death. Consider as well the holes left behind— the holes of suffering that we all have, the wounds and scars. And consider how nails are used to build and to rebuild a life. With the nails of Christ, we die with him. With the nails of Christ, a new life is built in and through him."

I reread ISO's email after I finished my draft of the Ash Wednesday meditation. He reminded me that I didn't need to tell him who I was even though we hadn't corresponded since last summer. He assured me he not only remembered me but said that our conversation had allowed him to let out a measure of personal grief. I pictured his grief like smoke billowing out of the fire burning up his old life.

He wrote: "I returned home for about six weeks in total before returning to America. I'm heading toward Texas to be near my niece and nephew. My five months of introspection and acceptance that the relationship with my wife had changed forever led me to resolve a new mission statement in life."

Mission statement—it was something I had assigned my parishioners to create that first summer I came to Church of the Mountain. "Write a life-focusing sentence," I said from the pulpit week after week. "What do you want your life to be about?" Condense the thousands of one's days, like thousands of pages, into a single sentence.

ISO shared his: "I want to be there for my niece and nephew until they graduate high school. This gives me a half-dozen years with them, and I can connect with them before they are lost to their teenage years. I fear they are already lost to their electronics, but I have a plan." He didn't say what his plan was, but being an engineer and all, I figured it had to be a well-thought-out one.

When we talked months ago, I recalled how the funeral ISO had attended with his mother left a hunger in him to connect with his sister's children and leave a legacy—from ashes to ashes, I thought—what remains no fire can destroy.

"It was a gift to be able to flip my personal perspective of being an engineer and chasing a career around the world to choosing uncle as my role and being content to earn money with any job in support of my mission statement."

He continued, "I yelled at God a lot on that journey. You and I discussed it a bit. My life has blissfully slowed down to two miles-per-hour since finishing, and I intend to keep it that way if at all possible. I am mindful that the associated sense of peace has removed me from my 'need for' faith recently. I'm in a transient place and hope (such a horribly unaccountable word) to find a church home when I get to Texas. That is the answer to your question of 'Where are you now?' A lifelong struggle to be sure."

MAUNDY THURSDAY

It had to do with feet, our hikers, ISO, and the mud time of year. I felt compelled to incorporate foot-washing into the Holy Thursday service, despite the grumblings I heard from others. "Word on the street is no one wants to come if you do that," one of my parishioners told me. But again, I felt strongly about doing it, no matter what, whether or not anyone else joined me. I would wash the feet of the elders. I would cup water in my hands for whoever came forward, open my fingers, and let the water trickle onto their feet and toes. I repeated the gesture before patting them with a dry towel and uttered the words, "Blessed are the feet of those who bring the good news."

On that Thursday evening, about thirty-five people came, most of whom participated in the ritual. I sat on the floor, and one by one, they came forward. The elders came first, barefoot, lifting one foot over the white enamel basin at a time—old feet, young feet, manicured feet, feet with thickened nails, and painted nails. The last one to come forward to my station was Andy, an elder. He rolled up his jeans, and as he lifted his right foot, I saw that he had painted his toenails, each one a different color.

"Jesus loves jokesters too," he said.

It was impossible to keep a straight face, and we chuckled. Then Andy told me he was going to wash my feet.

I hesitated, then lifted myself from the floor and sat in the chair. I extended my right foot first, grateful that I had had a pedicure days before. The metallic silver polish on my toes caught the light overhead. He held my heel, dipped his hands into the water, and poured it over me. The sensation of his hands flowing over my skin and bones, then rubbing the towel softly over my feet—it felt like light was being wrung from me. I do not know if this is how others experienced it, but there was something in the eyes of those as they moved away from the basin. It was as if the water that had been poured over their feet now flowed from their eyes.

Later, I texted Andy's wife and told her, "He missed a spot." It was an attempt to shake myself free of the feeling that perhaps only human touch accomplishes—the soothing of calloused hearts, the collapse of imaginary walls. I wondered if this was how hikers feel when they don't bathe for days, when they come to the hostel to shower—wilderness flowing over them from the inside out, the water holy and sacred, washing away all that doesn't matter.

GOOD FRIDAY

It seemed right that the skies were gray most of the day and rainy in part, with intermittent sun, as if grace was always trying to break through. I hadn't answered ISO back as of yet, as I suspected from his long delay in replying to me months later, that time and space were a required boundary. Considering his present condition of "not needing faith," he might not appreciate an immediate response. Now with Lent at an end, forty days later, there had been enough time between inquiries and answers.

Good Friday, as it's called, is an awful day, and on every one, I commit myself to be still for at least a chunk of time. Every time I do, I feel an earthquake tremor in the underground place inside me, a shift at my fault lines. I prayed: "Lord, into all the crevices and fractures of my being, come. Where I have fractured the heart of God, forgive me. Cause your spirit to flow over me like water and into all those broken places—cause me to overflow with all that you are; turn these places into lakes and rivers that run toward that heavenly sea."

Not sure what compelled me to share those words with ISO, not sure I know where that mystifying inner nudge came from, but since I had started Lent with him, I figured I could end it with him as well. Maybe it had to do with that photograph of ISO bowing his head, bending his knees at the summit of Katahdin. Perhaps it had something to do with that other mountain—Golgotha, the Place of Skulls. A life laid down, the grip uncurled, surrendered, the end of the trail.

MATRIMONY

*We are all travelers in the wilderness of this world, and
the best we can find in our travels is an honest friend.*

Robert Louis Stevenson

THE LATE APRIL MORNING WAS more winter than spring; the
wind blew gray and hard, swirling leaves and trees that creaked
like old arthritic men shivering in the cold. From a dark sky fell both
snow and freezing rain intermittently. Still, the air was alive with the
scent of living things; plants seduced to break through the muddy and
stiff ground on warmer days. A fragrant wood fire was burning somewhere not far away.

I was waiting at Lake Lenape, a small dammed lake on Mount
Minsi, only a short hike in from the trailhead in Delaware Water Gap.
My white stole flew up and out like the broken wings of a dove; my
hands froze inside my leather gloves as I paced to keep warm. It was
too cold to sit for long on the wooden bench near the water's edge.

The bride and groom were late; the bride texted me that they were
stuck in traffic. She hadn't yet told her groom of the wedding ceremony
that was about to take place on the trail, a truer place than a church or
any other venue for them. As far as he knew, they would marry on their
wedding day, planned for mid-May, a big event with dressy clothes
and friends and family by their sides. The wedding was still on, but
the marriage would happen today. No one else would know, just them.
Besides, the bride wanted to be married in their hiking clothes, which
she considered their second skin.

Audrey planned to venture out for a day hike, their favorite date, and I would be waiting for them at the lake. Her fiancé, Mark, had been a Ridge Runner for years, someone hired by the Appalachian Trail Conservancy to care for a section of the Trail. I wasn't sure he would be shocked since they had to apply for a marriage license and fill in the date. As I waited, other day-hikers passed by and offered to stand in as official witnesses for the wedding—the stole must have given it away. I thanked them but said it wasn't necessary since Pennsylvania's Quaker heritage doesn't require witnesses to participate or to sign the license.

Trees, forming archways overhead, would be their witnesses, as would the granite boulders and the waterfall, a stone's throw away. For me, and for them, this was a cathedral like no other. Nature provided crucifixes everywhere; the lake reflected the never-still heavens; there was a deep reverence. Droplets of freezing rain sounded like a distant choir, and the waterfall nearby provided a muted but impressive pipe organ, as well as damp incense.

About forty minutes later, Audrey and Mark arrived. Both were wearing down parkas, hiking pants, scarves, and winter caps, with daypacks slung over their shoulders. There was a hole in Mark's left sleeve at the elbow, duct-taped shut, but an occasional feather flew free from it, looking like the smallest of birds. He had an inkling of her scheme, he said.

Mark didn't stand much taller than Audrey, had a medium build, and looked to be a little older than she, probably in his late thirties. He wore a groomed beard and mustache, with a good share of gray in both. When he took off his cap before saying his vows, I saw his receding hairline, which made his face appear longer, more open. His hair had a soft downy look to it, like a baby's. He had sea-green eyes that could make you believe anything he said.

Audrey looked up at him adoringly, with a smile on her face that said she would never be unhappy again as she clutched his arm, laughing out loud at her well-thought-out plan. Her eyes were all the colors of a blue jay's wing against her thick red hair, tumbling out of her cap.

After Mark and I introduced ourselves, I suggested we begin. I threw my gloves onto the stones so I could turn the pages of what I had written.

"Audrey and Mark, you've come here today to immerse yourselves in the deep beauty and mystery of God's creation, to be restored and renewed by the trees, the air, and the waters—this is the perfect place for you to promise your life to each other . . .

"On this day, I ask God's blessing upon you. May you be strengthened for your life together and nurtured in your love for God. Life has its weather, its storms, its wind, which call us to grow deeper roots and to intertwine them in the invisible underground place where life and stability happen so that we might stay grounded. May you be an anchor not just for family, but for others too who have not yet found home, for love is not for marriage alone, but for every one of us . . ."

I read a passage from Ecclesiastes about how life is better when two go on a journey together to lift the other one up when one falls. It seemed appropriate for these two who regularly hiked into the wilderness, side-by-side, with no one else around. Then, I read a few lines from Elizabeth Barrett Browning's poem about how "Earth's crammed with heaven/And every common bush afire with God."

Weeks earlier, Aubrey told me their story and that Mark's trail name was Calm Water.

He was a non-anxious presence even when unexpected storms came with a wallop.

"You, Calm Water, maybe more than most, know the woods' power, the strength of hemlocks, the mystery of hidden springs. Here is your room with a view of what's called in Latin as the *mysterion tremendum*—'the mystery that causes us to tremble'—a beauty that causes us to shudder and challenges us to be transformed by its presence.

"You and Audrey have known each other for a long time. You grew up together, and now may you grow old together. May you walk through many forests and rest beside streams and waterfalls. May you be a restorative presence to each other. And may you both find and cling to the One who leads us all beside still waters and green pastures. May you hike the trail of your lives together, all the way to the end. May you find sanctuary in and with each other; may you bless one another all your days. I pray that every trail, every hemlock grove you find along the way, will lead you into a deep knowledge of God. May they lead you into a love for Him that has no boundaries, that nourishes you both in a way that nothing else compares, and that your love for one another is preparing you for."

They joined hands, faced each other, and repeated their vows. Mark kissed his bride, and I thought they froze together for a second. Afterward, they handed me a camera—they were both nature photographers—and I documented this moment in their lives, snapping photographs of them sitting on the bench by the lake, facing each other, kissing or holding each other tight. Hikers came by as if invited guests, congratulating the newlywed couple.

After I signed the license, they headed up the trail, through the woods of ancient oaks, toward the peak of Mount Minsi. They stopped to kiss every few yards, then linked arms, her head leaning against his shoulder. And the forest indeed did seem crammed with heaven—every tree, plant, and bush aflame with God.

FLIP-FLOPPING

Heaven knows we need never be ashamed of our tears, for they are rain upon the blinding dust of earth, overlying our hard hearts. I was better after I had cried, than before—more sorry, more aware of my own ingratitude, more gentle.

Charles Dickens

THE SUMMER OF 2016 WAS so hot and humid in the Northeast, much like the summers that followed. One could see the Delaware River evaporate into the sky, bare its rocks in the shallows that were once hidden by rapids, and expose the trees that slept on its bed. Fish stopped jumping, plunging deeper, swimming where the water was cooler, where the fingers of light could not grasp.

On the trail, even the shade of trees offered little relief; stalks of plants were brittle and broke easily, flowers struggled to bloom. Limestone and shale crumbled under one's feet, and the humidity wet the rocks, even as the cool streams that flowed down and across Mount Minsi were parched and drying up. Up and down the trail, water sources had vanished, leaving the hikers drained and thirsty and dangerously dehydrated by the time they struggled up the steep incline to the church, faces on fire, bodies pale, lips white.

Record numbers of hikers were expected that summer due to the film *A Walk in the Woods* premiering the summer before and *Wild* the year prior. As predicted, about fourteen hundred hikers reached Delaware Water Gap between April and August, and hundreds more were expected southbound in the fall. The park authorities had to jog groups of hikers, starting some at Harper's Ferry, West Virginia, and other groups from Springer Mountain, Georgia, which required a lot of flip-flopping (completing one part of the trail and returning to where one started to hike in the opposite direction. For example, starting from Harper's Ferry, hiking to Maine, then traveling back to Harper's Ferry and hiking to Springer Mountain).

Setting up for Thursday evening hiker feeds on the covered porch of Fellowship House throughout June, July, and August between four and five in the afternoon, in the height of the heat, was challenging enough as a skeletal crew, limp from the heat, wiped down the tables, started up the grill, and set up the tables. We never knew how many hikers would show up at six o'clock or how many church people would bring their offerings.

Gravity felt weightier in the humidity, the atmosphere airless; our lungs hurt. At six, after the church bells rang, the hikers lined up. You could see them swallow hard from all the saliva in their mouths flowing in anticipation of home-cooked food and a dedicated dessert table abundant with such sweet delights as blueberry pie, succulent watermelon, fresh cherries, and always homemade ice cream. More than one hiker who eyed the dessert table after heaping a plate full of main dish offerings admitted they were going to cry when they saw it. On average, we had anywhere between twenty and fifty hikers at every dinner, and somehow there was enough food to go around; we witnessed firsthand the miracle of "loaves and fishes" multiplying the meal every week.

On one exasperatingly hot July evening, I sat next to Wanderer, a man in his fifties who wore a black, tight-fitting nylon cap over his short gray-white hair, had an understated, recessed smile and slate-gray eyes. His plate overflowed with green salad, hot dogs, corn on the cob, chili, potato salad, shrimp cocktail, macaroni and cheese, and next to him, a bowl of homemade peach ice cream, melting at record speed. Wanderer was a French chef by vocation, owning a restaurant before being offered the opportunity to travel with a well-known rock group. He traversed the globe and traipsed around the country while serving up gourmet masterpieces for the band on tour. He showed me photographs of himself in a white chef's hat and shirt, standing in front of a table of his art, a still life of French pastries, dishes with flourishes, and garnishes of all kinds. Here he was now, though, the same man only different, ungarnished, wearing nylon shorts and a sleeveless t-shirt, smelling of anything but fresh-baked pastries.

"I'm hiking the trail out of penitence," he said. His words seemed to part the sea of conversation that was going on around us.

"What do you mean?" I asked.

"I was supposed to hike the Appalachian Trail the summer of 2017 with my fiancée. She was twenty years younger than me. I'm divorced, and I have a couple of grown children. Alice was the love of my life." The color of his eyes intensified as he choked back tears.

"What happened?"

"One day, she was working out in the gym when she bashed her leg against one of the machines. She finished working out before she went home, and she called me later that day, said she was having trouble breathing; I told her to go to the hospital. The next phone call I got was from my daughter telling me Alice had died. A blood clot had gone to her lungs from the injury she suffered earlier that day. She was gone." He paused, reconfigured his composure, "I'm walking for her. Everywhere I go, every shelter I stay in, I leave her notes, leave her a love letter in my entries; I write things I would have been saying to her if she were with me. Now I'm doing it alone. I always thought we would have the time. I'm trying to walk off the trauma of it all, hike into her absence, and a thousand miles in, I haven't been able to do it."

He described the AT as a "sufferfest," as pain, miles, hurt, cold, weather, mental anguish, all that never leaves you—unlike the love of his life whom he conjured up along the way, leaving notes such as "I didn't quit, I didn't let you down."

"I decided to hike the trail as a tribute to all the ones I've lost and reboot my life. I had been suffering crippling depression, and I needed to find a way to go on, and let me tell you, the trail's been grueling. I wouldn't have been able to do it without all the people who are supporting me, all the people I've met on the trail, people like those here at the church who provide such a great place for us to crash, and the trail angels; it's been an amazing experience."

"You said you were suffering crippling depression when you decided to hike the trail. Has hiking helped your depression?" I asked.

"I've learned that you change your life by changing your heart. I offered myself to the trail instead of to grief; I offered myself to adventure rather than to this paralysis grief left me in. I felt so guilty for not being with her, for her dying alone while I was off doing my thing. I want to forgive myself."

"Guilt and grief are difficult to separate, if not impossible," I said, "they keep flip-flopping. You think you are on the path toward healing when you find yourself on the trail of guilt."

"I have been saying a lot, been videotaping myself a lot. I don't want to leave anything unsaid to those I love so much and to those I've wronged. I want to make amends. I want to tell everybody who will listen if they aren't happy, if there's no passion in their life, they have to change it, 'cause life is too short to waste on mediocrity, you've got to be strong and fierce. I want to tell people, be the storm!"

He was naked in his grief and despair. His vocabulary of sorrow and regret tugged at the others who pretended not to hear, who side-glanced Wanderer as if they were afraid the raw sadness that clawed at him was contagious. Perhaps it was contagious, I thought, tearing away at the layers of others' sorrow and guilt, two things that most people want to avoid at all costs. They fill all the space around them instead with all sorts of noise and chatter so as not to hear their unuttered cries that rise like heat but fall like ice.

"Have you forgiven Alice for dying, for abandoning you, for leaving this life so young and so early?"

The question seemed to stun him. He looked out into the woods alongside the porch as if the trees might tell him what to say, as if the answer was somewhere outside himself—he had only to listen to hear it, something I expected he had practiced on his 1,000-mile hike here.

"I don't think I have," he said, bowing his head, lifting a forkful of food to his mouth, as if there was nothing more to say.

The windless evening brought little relief from the sultriness. Emptied plates were carried away. Hikers gathered afterward around the picnic table at the edge of the church property, smoked cigarettes, socialized, shared stories and laughter. Gravity seemed lighter with the incoming darkness as the crickets rubbed their wings together and trilled into the night.

Wanderer left a message to Alice in the hiker's journal before he left the next day:

Tribute to Alice: I'm so lost without you. I will find you in the next life. Wherever I am, you are with me. Love what you have before life teaches you to love what you have lost.

So typical of grief to insist on being a teacher.

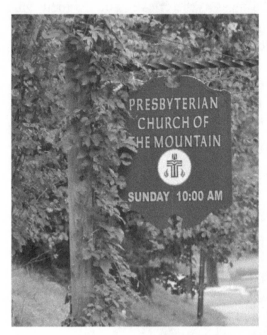

Presbyterian Church of the Mountain

Sign Welcoming AT Hikers

Cross alongside church,
welcoming all

Presbyterian Church of the Mountain, Delaware Water Gap, PA.
Home to the oldest, continuously-running hiker hostel on the
Appalachian Trail

Hikers serving themselves at the church's weekly Hikers Feed

Hikers chowing down before hitting the AT.

Larry Beck, Famous on the AT for his homemade ice cream at every Hikers Feed

Hikers Feed

David Childs and granddaughter Aliyah

Inside the Hikers Center's Bunkroom

Girls on the Trail

Driving up the church's steep driveway on a typical summer's day.

End of the Trail, Mount Katahdin, Maine

FORGIVENESS

Because forgiveness is like this: a room can be dank because you have closed the windows, you've closed the curtains. But the sun is shining outside, and the air is fresh outside. In order to get that fresh air, you have to get up and open the window and draw the curtains apart.

Desmond Tutu

I T WAS EARLY TUESDAY MORNING in July when I entered the center to find Lone Ranger sitting at a table in the corner of the common area. He was consulting his guide and AT map, scribbling numbers in his journal, deciphering the miles per day he'd have to walk to reach Katahdin before snow would close down the peak in Baxter State Park in Maine. Food was spread out in front of him, and gear piled around his feet. The other hikers had headed into town for breakfast and supplies. He was alone.

Everything about him was a shade of mahogany—his eyes, hair, sparse beard, and even the clothes he wore. I broke into his solitude to introduce myself.

After some conversation about how his hike was going, he confessed: "I don't know how to forgive. I keep trying. I'm trying to forgive myself and my wife, who didn't want to be married anymore. We were married for seven years. I loved her; I committed my life to her. I'm angry and hurt. I can't let go." The color of his eyes intensified as he spoke; he started to cry. There was a mountain of hurt in him that he couldn't summit.

Grief weighted the air.

It is a strange thing to think about how it is that two separate people, whole and complete in their own right, fall in love, commit to a life together, sign a legal contract of marriage, and become "one." When the relationship breaks, the two do not leave as they came into the union—they are fractured and incomplete. This severed, inexplicable human bond lives in the nerves, feeling like a phantom limb after an amputation, for the rest of one's life.

Lone Ranger had been divorced for only six weeks; his wife had had an affair, which ended the marriage. He lost his well-paying job a few weeks later, then decided to hike the AT within days, which explains why he had so late a start and had to calculate miles needed to hike per day to make Katahdin in time.

I knew from my own life that holding onto the hurt was a way to stay connected to the person, to the life once lived, to the past. How could I tell him that one day he would discover that there is in grief a deep beauty, a whiteness beneath the gray heaviness, an underground river of life beneath the sorrow?

After listening to the trauma of his recent past, and after he again asked how to forgive, I offered: "I too have known such brokenness. I know of only one way to live out forgiveness, to let go—it's the only thing that worked for me."

"What, what worked for you?"

"I hesitate to tell you, only because it's going to sound simple but impossible."

"Please," he pleaded.

"I started to find freedom in little bits and pieces only after I determined to pray for good for the person who hurt me so deeply, who betrayed me. It was the only way I could keep my heart from hardening. I'm not sure if it matters what your belief system is—whether you pray at all or believe in God. But for me, I too have needed to be forgiven, and I have needed to forgive myself," I said. "I see every day how anger and bitterness stop my blood from flowing."

Just then, another hiker walked into the center and intruded the conversation. He was lanky, in his early thirties, with a shaved head and a long black beard. He plopped down on the couch next to me, introduced himself as Evergreen, and reached out to shake our hands.

He missed not a syllable. Evergreen asked Lone Ranger, "Who is forgiveness for more —the person giving it or receiving it?"

Lone Ranger looked lost and confused; he shook his head. Before he could answer, other hikers entered the center. I asked him if he wanted to continue to talk, as I knew he was raw and vulnerable.

"Yes," he said. "No one talks about forgiveness on the trail."

Evergreen chimed in. "I was a broken person. I didn't want to forgive someone for what they did to me, but I found peace. I found a way to forgive, to be whole again."

I noticed the t-shirt Evergreen was wearing, one with a cross over his heart, and I knew immediately he was a Christian on a mission. Part of me recoiled. Too many well-meaning Christians don't listen; they want only to be heard, to convert. They don't sit still, let the other fill the space, or show any genuine desire to know the other.

"I'm not broken," Lone Ranger said. "I know I will survive this. The wound is fresh. We lost a child four years ago. If I can survive that, I will survive this."

He explained that, during his wife's pregnancy, the doctors discovered that his unborn child hadn't developed any kidneys in the fifth month of gestation. Then he learned he was the carrier of what's called Potter's Sequence.

"We made the most impossible decision. I watched my child, this life I helped to create— I watched his heart stop beating on the ultrasound. If I can live through that, I will survive this." Everything came pouring out of him—tears, groans, a gasp for air.

Then I asked, "Do you struggle with forgiving yourself for choosing to terminate the pregnancy?"

"No," he said. "It was an act of mercy."

I nodded. There was a pause. I wondered if it was unresolved grief that had come between him and his wife.

I was grateful that Evergreen didn't fill that moment of reverence with words.

"I'm agnostic and on my way to becoming an atheist," said Lone Ranger.

"I understand," was all I could say, knowing a loss often translates into the utter absence of any divine being or presence in the world.

Evergreen began sharing again that he also understood how Lone Ranger might conclude that either there was no God, or if there was a God, He wasn't worth knowing. Such a God asked too much of the very creation he created.

Lone Ranger stood up rather abruptly, noting he needed to hit the trail as the morning was slipping away. It was nearly noon by then. He shuffled about, gathering and packing the few things still spread out on the table, before muttering a quick goodbye.

Evergreen followed me to my office and sat down on the loveseat for a good half an hour. He reminded me that he and his team from Youth with a Mission had been at the church and Hikers Center two years earlier. Once again a team of young adults was traveling up and down the AT, providing trail magic for any hiker who passed by, offering food, candy, and cold drinks. I confess I did not remember him, but I did remember the YWAM van parked at the church for a couple of nights back then. It had been my first summer here, and there were many "unforgettable" people I couldn't conjure up two years later.

We walked to the local cafe, ordering red pepper and grilled chicken sandwiches and cups of coffee. I asked him what he was referring to when he had spoken to Lone Ranger about forgiving others, what story he would have told had him if he had had the time.

"I was sexually abused when I was two by my babysitter. My parents figured it out when I reacted certain ways."

"Do you remember it?" I asked.

"I have one memory. But when my brother was born when I was three, I wasn't allowed to play with him my entire childhood. My parents were afraid that I would do to him what had been done to me. I wasn't even allowed to be alone in the same room with him, so I never really bonded with him the way brothers do."

What struck me at that moment was the generous nature of this young man, his exuberance and candor, friendliness and fearlessness toward anyone who walked by our table, despite what he said next.

"My innocence was stolen. Then I was guilty my whole life. I haven't been able to trust. I have had to fight all my life the lie that it was my fault, that I was faulty, and that I was to blame."

I listened as he continued—he hadn't had any relationship with the opposite sex that lasted more than a few months. His younger brother, the one with whom he was forbidden to bond while growing up, loved to dress up in girl's clothes, and Evergreen suspected that maybe his now grown-up brother was gay.

"My parents are really struggling with this," he said, his voice full of compassion. He paused before saying, "I've come to believe single-ness is a gift."

He had been a prisoner of lurid expectations, I thought. Yet, there was something very safe about him with his toned-down sexuality and his amped-up sincerity. Celibacy was not a curse, but a choice, and with it came clarity and freedom for this charismatic young man to pursue his purpose and his mission, at least at this time in his life.

"I can focus on what is before me without distraction. I'm not sure, but maybe God has called me to be single for the rest of my life, and I am good with that."

We talked some more about his family of origin, how his parents' fears had shaped him. When he was a young man, he had what he called a similar experience as had the fictional main character, Shasta, in C.S. Lewis's *The Horse and His Boy*, one book in The Chronicles of Narnia series.

"Shasta was walking in a deep woods," Evergreen said, retelling the story. "He was alone, he was frightened, it was dark, and he could see nothing when all of a sudden he sensed someone walking beside him. Shasta asks: 'Who are you?' The presence alongside him says, "'One who has waited long for you to speak.' That was what happened to me. One day I realized I wasn't alone, and I had never been alone. It changed everything. Forgiveness came almost immediately for the woman who had abused me and for my parents."

Sometime later, I left Evergreen at the trailhead in Delaware Water Gap with his team hanging out in front of tables full of goodies. As we hugged goodbye, he said to me, "You can't out-give God."

* * *

As the afternoon wore on, I couldn't help but reflect upon the conversations I'd had with Lone Ranger and Evergreen: how sexual intimacy has both the power to create life and steal it away, how there is in the sexual encounter the mystery of skin hunger, the total exposure of one's self, a complete lack of defense, the ultimate cry for acceptance, and the expectation of tender mercies.

Various people have shared their stories of childhood sexual abuse with me over the years. It seems as though the maps of their lives were torn to shreds, and they have had to spend a portion of their days either piecing it together or drawing up a new one. Such trauma often destroys the willingness, or perhaps the ability, to trust another person again. Even with the most casual sexual encounter, there is a grafting that takes place in the most invisible spaces as each becomes part of the other's marrow. I can't think of much else that can be as mysterious and powerful, both a blessing and a curse.

WINGS

Even the youths may faint and grow weary, and young men stumble and fall. But those who wait upon the LORD will renew their strength; they will mount up with wings like eagles; they will run and not grow weary; they will walk and not faint.

Isaiah 40:31
New International Version

EAGLE DESCENDED UPON THE CHURCH on a Monday afternoon in June. He had named himself Eagle, for he had walked and not grown weary on the AT. He had fallen and crashed years before, he confessed. Slender and soft-spoken, he exuded a broken-wing kind of humility. He was in his early fifties, with short, silky brunette hair. He carried himself like someone who had been successful in life, all tidy and well-groomed. His hazel-green eyes were translucent, and I felt like I could see into him.

He was a rich man who worked himself to the bone, living in a home with copper gutters in an affluent town in New England. He lost it all in a divorce and was a recovering alcoholic. He was free, he said, soaring high now. The desire for wealth, materialism, and success was below him, growing smaller and more meaningless. He flew higher than ever before.

Eagle joined a small group of parishioners and me for Bible study that night, sitting outdoors around a table on the back porch. It was one of those evenings that made you want summer to last forever with its late-setting sun and lengthening shadows. Oxygen-rich breezes blew the scent of trees over us—pines, oaks, poplars—while June bugs buzzed and congregated around lights.

"I've had a non-stereotypical mid-life crisis," he explained. "Instead of falling in love with a younger woman, I'm working on falling in love with myself. I had a Damascus Road experience while on the trail; a brilliant light came through the trees. I was knocked off my feet."

He referred to the famous biblical story when Saul, a Jewish religious leader and persecutor of the early church, ordered the killing of Christ's followers. On his way to Damascus, a brilliant light blinded him, and he fell from his horse when he heard Jesus say, "Saul, Saul, why are you persecuting Me?" It was that moment when Saul became Paul, a believer in the resurrected Jesus as the Son of God, a moment that changed the entire course of his life.

"I was walking on the trail when I was overcome with this revelation of God, of what my life is supposed to be about, how I am to live, that God is real. All I want to do is bring love, show love, and share my transformation," he said.

I witnessed him earlier that day doling out portions of food and epiphanies to fellow hikers.

"God is more important than anything or anyone, even family," he said.

I watched Roger, one of those gathered around the table, as Eagle spoke those words. Roger had lost a son two years earlier in a car accident, hit by a drunk driver. Six months before losing his son, both of his legs were amputated above the knee after having suffered sepsis from pneumonia. When Roger was a young man, he had lost his spleen in a car accident, and he couldn't fight the infection as others could have. He married the nurse who cared for him thirty-five years ago; she was sitting next to him.

"I had a Damascus Road experience, too," Roger said. "When I was in the hospital in a coma after my legs were amputated, I was being chased by demons. The staff found me on the floor that night. I remember running from dark screaming creatures, and I woke a transformed man."

"It's about love, nothing less; there is nothing more," said Eagle.

"I've walked over a thousand miles; I have no fat to spare, but my heart has grown big and full. My clothes are full of holes; my boots have worn out, I am exhausted, depleted, but in such a way that I am filled all the more."

He had sold his lucrative business after his divorce to be unencumbered, he said.

"Do you have children?" Roger asked.

"Yes, two—ages thirteen and fifteen."

I believed everything he said and everything that he didn't say—that his family had lost him while he found love for himself, the power of less, and the exuberance of exhaustion at the end of a long day's hike. He had taken flight.

GEOGRAPHY OF SUFFERING

*We shall draw from the heart of suffering itself the
means of inspiration and survival.*

Winston Churchill

T WENTY-SEVEN-YEAR-OLD MALE HIKER, TRAIL NAME Okie
Dokie, had a deep-toned, staccato laugh and a hospitable face, by
which I mean he had room for anyone and everyone in his line of vision at any present moment. His abundance of wooly facial hair spread
out across his face so much that I had to search for his walnut-colored
eyes. Like most hikers who have traveled a thousand miles to arrive
here, his body was more bone than flesh. A book lay open on his lap,
and sections of *The New York Times* were fanned out on the couch next
to him.

"Haven't heard that trail name before. How'd you get it?" I asked.

"I was talking on the phone to a friend back home, and when the
guy I was walking with heard my friend call me my nickname, Okie
Dokie. The name stuck."

"So everything is always alright with you?" I asked, both of us
chuckling. "I can't tell you how nice it is to find a hiker reading *The
New York Times*."

"I'm a news junkie, probably because I majored in International
Relations at college," he said with a hint of joviality. "I'm used to read-
ing several papers a day, listening to the BBC, and any program except
Fox or CNN; I find American news is skewed and places us at the

center of the universe. I haven't immersed myself in what's happening around the world as much since I've been on the trail. I kind of miss it and I kind of don't. It's been good to take a leave of absence from it all; it's like going through a culture cleanse," he said.

"I imagine the trail is good for that; it gives space to think about other things," I said, sitting on an adjacent couch.

"I see a lot of hikers with headphones on and walking in groups. They miss stuff; there's always something going on around you, some rustling, birds singing, owls screeching, acorns falling from trees, all kinds of music."

"Silence can be terrifying for some," I said. "I know there have been many times in my life when that was true for me."

He nodded as if he related to what I said. "I listen to books once in a while. I just finished listening to the books *Wild* and the most recent *Game of Thrones,*" he said. He moved the book from his lap onto the couch next to *The New York Times*, with its spine pressed open. "I miss Maine where there are no cars, no noise pollution. From New York onwards, all you hear is civilization. Crossing over the Delaware River on the bridge between New Jersey and Pennsylvania, all you can focus on is the traffic, and you smell nothing but car exhaust."

"A little too much reality, right, after being on the trail?" I asked. "What made you decide to hike the AT?"

"I always wanted to do it but wasn't sure I could. The longest back-packing trip I'd ever gone on lasted a week, and I wasn't carrying a fifty-pound pack days on end. I don't have a family of my own, I don't own a house, I have a job I can go back to, so I figured this was a good time. I've pretty much been a workaholic."

"Now, you're a walkaholic," I said, as I sensed he was running toward himself, not away.

He continued, "A friend of mine's brother died last year while rid-ing his bike on the streets of Las Vegas. He was young and had just started his own bicycle business." His tone softened, and his speech slowed; he turned his eyes away from mine. "Everyone always says they'll do such and such later in life, but then something happens. They get sick, or they get killed, or they can't do what they want, for one reason or another. One of my friends had hiked the AT; she put the notion of hiking the trail into my head. I also wanted to test myself, as I'm transitioning into a different career; I wanted to see if I could commit myself to it. I just finished taking a training course to become a geo-medic before I came out on the trail."

"A geo-medic? Sounds exotic, love the name, but what is it?" I asked.

"It's a medic who goes where there's been a disaster, like Haiti's earthquake in 2010. The course I took was in wilderness medicine training. It prepares medics to handle disease outbreaks and provide care in remote settings in developing nations. It taught how to do different medical treatments that doctors typically perform, like sutures and intubation, those kinds of things."

As he spoke, I recalled the images broadcast over the news of the earthquake in Haiti, of burning bodies, collapsed homes, people wandering the broken streets, children searching for mothers and fathers. We witnessed horrible things we could do nothing about, except to send money that everyone knew was as likely not to reach the victims as it was to reach them; some joined volunteer rescue teams or mission trips to help. All of us stared and ached and bled inside, experiencing the damage, fear, and loss from afar. We took the fractured world into ourselves. We participated in the Haitians' suffering in this strange, mystical way.

"That's one of the reasons I'm out here on the trail," he continued. "I need to test myself. After majoring in International Relations, my passion for learning about other cultures grew. I began to travel to different places and see firsthand how people live differently. Half of Africa is at war. There is unrest and violence everywhere. You see how people are being abused every day; thirty-plus conflicts are going on around the globe, although Americans don't hear about them. I wanted to see the world for myself, so I went to China in 2009, then to Bangkok, and traveled through the rest of Thailand two years later, where I lived with Buddhist monks for six weeks. I wanted to experience an ancient culture. Traveling is what got me interested in working with humanitarian aid and becoming a geo-medic." He shifted his weight, fiddled with the pages of the downturned book. "What I learned from the monks is that life is suffering, no matter what, and you should help people. You need to do things to ensure good karma."

"Is that why you want to be a geo-medic, to ensure good karma?"

"Yeah, I think so, even though I consider myself an atheist, to tell you the truth. I grew up Catholic, attended Catholic schools my entire life, and found Christianity too judgmental."

"Human nature is judgmental; everyone wants to believe they are better than someone else. Jesus only judged the self-righteous, never the humble. Being a geo-medic is an outstanding example of practicing true religion, in my view." I said, suddenly aware of the Syrian refugees' faces staring up from *The New York Times* front page, eyes begging for help, tongues silent, yet I could hear their cries. "Maybe we're all trying to work out our salvation in one way or another, even if we don't name it. I'm not an atheist because we're capable of offering mercy and compassion to another human being. For me, that's proof God exists and that we're made in His image."

"Never really thought about it in that way," he said, and then he seemed to recede into himself as if he were suddenly walking alone in the woods. I wasn't sure if he was pondering what was said or simply wanted not to talk about faith.

I glanced out the window at the trembling golden leaves, aware that I had lived thirty years more than he had. The conversation turned toward small things then, where the towels were for showering, numbers to call for rides into town, and local places to eat. As I stood up to leave, I wanted to say that it's suffering that pried me open to receive all that is beautiful in this life, but I knew he had to learn that on his own; maybe he already knew.

GOD WHO ASKS
TOO MUCH

When I lay these questions before God I get no answer.
But a rather special sort of "No answer." It is not
the locked door. It is more like a silent, certainly not
uncompassionate, gaze. As though He shook His head
not in refusal but waiving the question. Like, "Peace,
child; you don't understand."

C.S. Lewis

S OMETIMES IT JUST SEEMS LIKE God asks too much, even of
those who don't offer themselves. Christianity forbids child sacrifice, and yet I fear missionaries have done so on the altar of duty. At
least that is what I thought until thru-hiker, The Scientist, proved me
wrong.

In July 2015, a local television crew came to the Church of the
Mountain to film one of the Thursday night hikers potluck dinners,
highlighting the hostel, the hikers, and the church people. The segment
would run on public television throughout August. During dinner, I met
The Scientist, a twenty-one-year-old recent Christian college graduate
who had grown up in Pakistan, the son of missionaries. From second
grade on, he was sent to boarding school three hours away from his
parents. His father was a Presbyterian minister, and his mother an ob-
stetrician and gynecologist serving a mission hospital.

When he told me this, so many memories surfaced of my two-
week trip to Pakistan in March of 1994, traveling with photographer

Joe Guerriero to document a story that we had pitched to *Life* magazine. We landed in Lahore and stayed there for several days as guests of Prince Jaffar, a member of the royal Leghari family, whose cousin was Pakistan's president at the time. Together with the prince and his entourage, we traveled from Lahore to the capital of Islamabad, where I met Benazir Bhutto and later interviewed President Farooq Leghari. We continued to Baluchistan, to Fort Monroe, and the family palace in Choti. My recollections of the country were of warm hospitality, tribal life, and disconcerting tribal warfare; of an ancient feudal system within a parliamentary government where villagers bowed before the prince, touching his feet, casting their eyes downward, pleading their cause. Prince Jaffar was a savior. There were men in turbans with henna-stained beards and hands, young boys working in cotton factories late into the night; rusty razors clasped in crippled hands on the village streets as barbers hawked their skills with one hand and pliers in the other for any teeth that needed pulling. In the marketplace, skinned and putrefying chickens hung in the open air, exposed to sunlight, for villagers to purchase.

Pakistan was a dry and dusty place, the ground sun-scorched and waterless, even in the mountains when we traveled to the British Fort Monroe, as it was the season before the rains. One day, when we were descending the mountains in Dera Ghazi Khan District of Punjab, where Fort Monroe is located, a fast-moving rainstorm passed through the mountains and flooded a dry riverbed. Prince Jaffar commandeered a stranger's jeep, and his driver drove us across it, only to be swept a distance downstream. We had an armed escort everywhere we went, but not at night when we were at their residence, or guest houses, or at the Marriott that would suffer a terrorist attack a few years later.

On one occasion, at night, while staying in a guest house in Islamabad, one of the village men peered into the bathroom window while I was dressing for bed. I let out a startled yelp, and I ran for cover and stayed on the couch in the photographer's room. Being female, a foreigner, and the only white woman many of the Pakistanis had ever seen, I often felt on display and vulnerable among the curious men. While in Choti, home to the ancestral Leghari palace, I went beyond the palace walls to the village tailor to be measured for a salwar kameez, the traditional outfit for men and women. A pact of children followed me in the streets where ruts of raw sewage ran and stank in the heat. I saw a few older kids in the distance bathing in a muddy puddle of water. Soon men and women followed and crowded around the tailor's kiosk. They giggled as the tailor stretched his measuring tape across my chest and arms without touching me. I was the show. By the end of the day, he had sown the garment and delivered it.

Pakistan, which means "Land of the Pure" in Urdu, and its people, touched me so profoundly it left a scar with its deep poverty, the unmerciful desert, and the tribal discord. Growing up in such a country as The Scientist had, growing up anywhere, the perspective must be different than someone merely passing through, even a journalist who attempts to understand, to be immersed, who suffers a culture shock that never really goes away.

The Scientist said, "My mother delivered eight thousand babies a year at the mission hospital." His voice was all shiny and glowed like copper. "I was so blessed to have my parents. Even when I was hours away, I knew that my sister and I were their top priority. I liked being with my friends."

He earned the trail name The Scientist as he hoped to be a science teacher. Tall and thin, like most hikers with this much mileage under their belt, he wore a reddish-blond beard, kind of scraggly, and had cobalt blue eyes. There was a wholesomeness to him and a sturdiness, not so much physically, but a steadfastness and strength of character, and an innocence.

"You are different from a lot of young male hikers who pass through here," I said. "Most of them don't speak of their parents, or when they do, they don't talk so kindly about them, as you have. It strikes me because they sent you off to boarding school at such a young age." I shared with him how my aunt and uncle had been Baptist missionaries in Niger, where they raised their four children. After many years of being tutored at home by their mother, each child was eventually sent away to boarding school. None of my cousins seemed to resent being sent away to the Ivory Coast. The cousin closest to my age had a high school graduating class of eight.

"My girlfriend isn't Presbyterian, but of the Eastern Orthodox faith tradition," he added. "I'm investigating joining her church."

"Are your parents supportive of the possibility of your switching churches?"

"They are okay with it."

Because of the film crew, and a lot going on around us, it was challenging to talk one on one, but I wanted to ask him if he called Pakistan home or the United States since he was rooted in this foreign country so early in life. I never got the chance to ask. I didn't want to focus on him only as others were sitting near us.

An older gentleman of small stature, in his late fifties, wore glasses that magnified his eyes. Every time I looked at him, it was like being stared at through binoculars at close proximity. His trail name was The Pharmacist. I guessed he had squinted at too many chemical formulas and small print that no one reads. His white beard was short and groomed; he had a pearl white complexion and a smile that swallowed everything around it. He said he was from Kansas, a flat terrain, no training possible at home before coming on the trail.

"I'm a runner. It didn't help me when it came to hiking," he said. He paused for a moment and then said something as if he had needed to say it for a long time: "Know what I've learned on the trail? That everything I was looking for on the trail I discovered I had at home. I'm going home knowing I never have to look elsewhere."

Next to The Pharmacist was Tiger Mike, who confessed to being half-Portuguese and half-German, a romantic and a stoic.

"What about the story of your life?" I asked.

"It's a long, boring story."

"No such thing," I said.

"I'm about to retire as a police captain from a small city in New England, and I'm using up my sick days by hiking the trail," Tiger Mike said.

At that, the three of them began to discuss what they did for a living. It was the first time they delved into the subject since having walked together for some distance. That struck me, since off the trail, it might be one of the top five questions one person asks when getting to know another. What work a person does gives a clue to how they spend their days, what difficulties they might face, obstacles overcome, level of education, etc. Tiger Mike and The Pharmacist were retiring, and The Scientist was about to start his career. What became clear to me is that what a person does for a living and their socioeconomic status meant nothing on the trail. These categories, or dividing lines, didn't exist on the AT.

"If you can walk the trail, you can do anything," Tiger Mike said.

Later that evening, a few of us gathered at the Deer Head Inn for a night of improvisational jazz—anyone can join in, and sometimes hikers do, taking a turn at the piano, bass, or drums. Tiger Mike was there and spoke to me briefly whenever there was enough silence to hear each other before later slipping out to the front porch to light up a cigar.

"Everyone has a vice," he said, puffing away.

I pulled out a chair opposite him at the small metal table and sat down, glancing out upon the street, inhaling jasmine and honeysuckle. The jam session continued, but tonight there was too much noise for me and being outside was a relief.

"I'm walking the trail to raise funds for a child advocacy group back home," he said. "I couldn't see the point of walking the trail for no reason. I saw this as a way to connect with an organization that is of profound importance to our community. I've seen the most heinous crimes committed against the most vulnerable. I want to use this trek in the woods to bring attention to this. It's one of my passions." He leaned back in the metal chair and continued to puff away at his cigar, blowing the heavy smoke away from me.

Maybe it was his job in law enforcement that forced him to witness and rescue children who were victims of abuse, or maybe, I thought, there was more to his long story that he didn't want to share. For some, divulging the hardest story to tell lightens the darkness.

"Heck of a way to use up your sick days, huh? People come to the hostel broken and scarred and bruised and healthier than they've ever been and may ever be again. I know there is something that happens out there in the woods that is beyond explanation."

"Long-distance hiking takes everything out of you, and then, somehow, it puts it all back in, only in a different order," said Tiger Mike.

Maybe the God who asks too much knows exactly what He is doing.

GOSPEL AND GUNS

Be strong, courageous, and firm; fear not nor be in terror before them, for it is the Lord your God who goes with you; He will not fail you or forsake you.

Deuteronomy 31:6
Amplified Bible

A MAN WEARING CAMOUFLAGE PANTS AND shirt, a backward baseball cap, with wavy aging hair left notes at the Hikers Center. One note, two pages long in a legible script, was addressed to no one. On it, he had scribbled his social security and phone numbers, that he was straight, and a confession: "I killed a man, but he sexually abused a child."

The first time he came to the church, I was away on vacation; the police were called, but Sam, as we later learned his name, was nowhere to be found by the time the officer arrived. Our local police force clocked only about ten hours a week in the Gap, so we had to wait for the state police. David passed Sam's jottings on to the troopers. As far as we knew, Sam was homeless, living under a nearby bridge, or in a park, or the cemetery a few blocks away—at least that is where people said they had spotted him when he wasn't walking through the Gap day after day. Walking, he seemed to leave a trail of ghosts behind him, haunting those he encountered on his way so that no one could name what stormed in their gut when he was close, when their senses bolted into high alert. He felt dangerous, unpredictable, and out of control, even to those unaware of his written confessions.

He landed at the center once every few days to shower. Other hikers reported that he spoke unintelligibly as if tearing random words from sentences and stringing them together in an invisible one-person game of Scrabble. He smelled of damp earth and mildew, not unlike the hikers. The police were called several more times before the church filed a formal complaint.

Sam stopped coming to church once the complaint was filed, until months later when someone gave me a note left in the church's nursery, written on a paper napkin with all the personal information on it again, but this time with no confession of murder. I figured he left it when he had attended an AA meeting on the previous Sunday evening held in Fellowship House, even though the complaint was still in effect. I called the police again to notify them, but I never heard if they followed through. No more notes were found over the next several weeks.

That same summer, only a few days after the complaint had been filed, another man showed up mid-worship service carrying a black bag. He walked to the front of the church, sat down, squirmed, and shifted his black bag here and there, adjusting the elastic waistband of his sweat pants a little too frequently, fidgeting every few seconds. At first, I thought he was a hiker, but everyone's eyes fastened to him, trying to discern if the black bag concealed a weapon. Many congregants later disclosed they stopped listening to the sermon after he arrived, convinced the man was out to harm.

The thirty-something-year-old wore his dark hair slicked back, had hard-boiled facial expressions, and a fast-paced New Yorker tongue. He lingered after church, speaking with me until everyone had left and we were alone. He rambled on, straying from one subject to the next without any thread tying them together; he admitted that he had been thrown out of several towns in Pennsylvania. His name was Evan, he said, and he had lots of money, yet he was living at a motel down the street that had a reputation for drugs and a suspicion of prostitution and human trafficking. Said he was thinking of buying the million-dollar motel that was up for sale (days later, he asked one of our members for thirty-five dollars and a ride into New York City) since he had been a successful stockbroker and had once worked for the "Wolf of Wall Street."

That evening, he showed up for the jazz concert on the church lawn, helping to carry equipment from Fellowship House down the steps to the gazebo in the side yard, inserting himself into the community a little too vigorously, it seemed to me. The following Thursday, he came to the Hikers Feed, this time with his nine-month-old son and a teenage-looking Asian wife in tow. Evan dictated what she could eat since she was breastfeeding and when she could breastfeed their son. She was tall and thin with waist-long black hair, dressed in a short, lacy summer dress and wide-brimmed straw hat. It was clear they came to feed themselves, not others. Evan told me he knew his "wife" for one day before marrying her; I was suspicious, could she have been trafficked or a mail-order bride?

Both Sam and Evan left us feeling as if there was a wolf at the door, and we were nothing more than little pigs inside, feasting on the Word of God. Their disruptive presence also struck me as a test of how Christian charity and common sense were to be practiced. On several occasions, I had seen Sam and Evan walking together through town. The Session (the Presbyterian leadership of the church) was divided on how to proceed. At first, there was more battle than balance. I reminded the elders that I was alone at church day in and day out, engaging with those who pretended to be hikers but suffered some mental instability. And being a woman, I felt more vulnerable than most men might understand. Admitting such, I felt like a phony—where was my faith?

Our church could no longer do business as usual, as there had been too many incidences of violence in churches around the country. A young man opened fire at a Bible study in the South, killing more than he left alive. Preachers were being murdered at their pulpits. The most dangerous times in church are March and April, which I assumed had more to do with the resurrection than not as if killing a preacher or two would disprove the resurrection of Jesus Christ.

On Session was a recently retired FBI analyst whose intuitive sense was much sharper than the rest of ours. Conflict ensued. I knew a few parishioners had a license to carry a firearm; I didn't know if they packed while attending worship service. How could we be, as the Bible taught, "Shrewd as serpents, innocent as doves"?

I felt unprepared yet responsible for my Session and for the safe-keeping of the hikers who sought shelter here and for my flock. My white-Anglo-Saxon-Protestant middle-class upbringing left me bewildered and wanting to believe the best about others.

It seemed apparent that Sam suffered from a form of schizophrenia. Had he committed a crime because someone had violated him, or was it guilt or shame that deformed his life? Who could discern what was reality and what was fantasy?

Ironically, I had been preaching from lectionary passages that were all about demon possession and Christ's deliverance. Demons were thought to be responsible for bizarre, often violent, behavior in ancient times. Most modern-day followers of Christ would attribute the unexplainable to mental illness, not demonic possession. Supernatural strength, foaming at the mouth, indecipherable syllables, extreme fluctuations of mood—all were attributed to an evil force which had one intent—to destroy the possessed and those around them. The most common demonic experience I have witnessed in my lifetime, this day and age, has been drug and alcohol addiction.

So what does it take—both gospel and guns?

In time, the dust settled on the congregation. Evan continued to come to church, always too late, as if to make a spectacle with baby and wife in tow, sans black bag. Suspicion had not slipped away, however, although it did dull in time. A month or so into their stay at the local inn, Evan's wife, Mei-Mei, attended Bible study. Sweet-faced and shallow-voiced, a willow of a young woman, she never let her son out of her grasp. He slept in her lap the entire time, his face in the crook of her neck, sharing the same breath.

On the hottest of summer days, Evan forbade Mei-Mei to leave the motel room so that the management couldn't throw them out.

She was a prisoner, she told someone at church. She also said that her husband had brought another man into their bed, wanting her to have sex with him. During a phone conversation with Mei-Mei, I told her she could leave him, even though he held her "citizenship" papers over her head. Women's Resources, which helps those trapped in abusive relationships, would help her with everything she needed, including legal aid. Mei-Mei wanted to go back to China, but she wouldn't leave her son behind.

Meanwhile, our FBI retiree worked on a security plan. It was mostly basic stuff to look out for, but she came up with specific codes so others would know there was a concern among us.

By summer's end, Evan and Mei-Mei went back to New York City, at least for a short time, and they were living in a homeless shelter, according to one of our church members. He was seen on and off again around town in the months that followed, but I never saw Mei-Mei again, nor do I know what happened to her and their son. I learned later that Evan had it out for me after I told him we needed to close up the building following a Monday night Bible study. He insisted on staying so his wife could nurse their son. I told him she was welcome to sit outside on the covered porch—it was a warm night.

In reading hikers' blogs, a few hikers announced that they were on the AT to raise awareness and funds for research into mental illness because another hiker had walked into the woods, only to abandon all his gear and thousands of dollars. His family and park rangers were forced to search for him up and down the trail.

Madness, the word itself once used to characterize mental illness, suggests out-of-control anger that disorders and deranges the mind. It lets no light into the uncertain darkness that resides in us all, revises what others see as real and true, like a fever that melts and reshapes all it sees.

I don't know if "demons" are expelled on the trail, if for every step a person treads, a destructive spirit is trampled upon, flattened, and left behind. I don't know if there is a spiritual cleansing that comes with physical exhaustion or if the creative spirit that breathes in us all surfaces with great exertion. But I know that when the life-giving spirit within all is held hostage by something, some event or someone, it fights to the death and sometimes loses.

HOLY AND UNHOLY
ANGELS

"You are fettered," said Scrooge, trembling.
"Tell me why?"

"I wear the chain I forged in life," replied
the Ghost.

"I made it link by link, and yard by yard; I
girded it on of my own free will . . ."

Charles Dickens

T HEY ARE KNOWN AS TRAIL angels. They appear as if out of the
thinnest of air. These individuals show up at various locations
along the AT with glistening cold bottles of water, icy beer, dry cigarettes, homemade sandwiches, and other delights. Sometimes these
angels lug a barbecue grill to a trailhead, cooking up hamburgers and
hot dogs over smoldering coals. Hikers muster up the strength to run
like ancient priests toward these burnt offerings, indulging in what is
called trail magic. Some trail angels open their homes or backyards
for hikers to have a place to lay their heads for a night or two. These
angels, who specialize in stranger generosity, emerge on trails all over
the United States—on the Pacific Crest Trail, the Continental Trail, and
the Appalachian Trail.

On one Sunday evening, two young men drove up the church driveway, disembarked their vehicle, carrying several six-packs of beer and

a couple of cigarette cartons. I thought this was more black magic than trail magic, especially since the church doesn't allow any alcoholic beverages on the premises—and all the AT guidebooks are clear about this. I told the young men they couldn't bring their donations into the Hikers Center, so they promptly left and found other places in town to share their sacrifices.

The following evening, a young woman came to me after dark, seeking someone to talk to outside her hiking group and who didn't know the man she had fallen in love with while hiking the trail. In her mid-twenties, she was a pretty girl with long strawberry-blonde hair that she had the habit of compulsively twirling into locks between her fingers that earned her the name Twirl. We sat outside where the moonlight's sheen made her skin look like mother-of-pearl.

She told me who she was by the choices she had made, by the path she had followed, graduating from college a couple of years earlier, then left her job as an elementary school teacher after two years, discontent with her choice of careers. She had met, and fallen in love with, a young man on the AT; they had been hiking together for the last three months. Words like gregarious, kind, fun-loving, caring, and leader were how she described the man called Rocky.

"He was walking the trail as part of his recovery from addiction," she said. "He was doing really well; we got along great. A few days ago, we got into town and stayed at the motel around the corner when he asked someone in the parking lot for heroin. He bought some, then snorted it, said it was so good, he had to buy more.

"The next day we met a woman and her husband at the local diner who offered to bring us to their house and put us up for the night and cook for us. She told us how her daughter once walked the AT, and so she was now extending hospitality to other hikers. I wasn't sure about going home with these strangers, but we went anyway. I thought it might be a good idea to get away from where we were staying and the guy who sold him the heroin. We had our bedroom upstairs by ourselves in their house, and we took showers, ate an amazing meal, and then Rocky went up to lie down.

"I went up an hour later. He was blue, foaming at the mouth. I was so scared." Her voice trembled. "I was so afraid to tell the woman and her husband, but I couldn't wake him. I shook him; I tried everything. I called down to her, and she called the ambulance. Now he's in the hospital. He almost died, and the doctors say he might have to be on dialysis for the rest of his life."

I let her talk, and twirl, and hear herself, then asked, "What do you want to do now?"

"I want to go and say goodbye to him and keep walking the trail. I thought we might be together forever before now, but I can't be with him. I feel terribly guilty like I shouldn't leave him, and I talked to his parents, and I think they feel that way too, that I should stick around and be there for him. But, he's been to rehab many times, and he's been going to college for the last ten years. Rocky's thirty years old."

"You aren't responsible for him, you know," I said. "You will never be able to save him, even though it seems like love should do that. You can't be responsible for his life or his recovery."

She talked some more. I listened to her reason her way through an emotional maze, trying to find the way through and out of the place she found herself in. I wanted to share with her about my daughter, who has struggled with addiction, how it is a choice a person makes, and once they choose their drug or drink, it is exclusive; there's no room for anyone or anything else. I thought Twirl was right to walk away. I understood his parents' desire for her to stay and be by his side, but hadn't he made a choice not to be hers when he copped dope from an unholy angel in a parking lot? I know of little else that is as demonic as drug addiction—it destroys the addict's life and threatens to destroy everyone who loves him or her. I wanted to say, "Run for your life," but I resisted.

Earlier that same evening, a good-looking, fair-haired young man had walked into the Hikers Center while I was inside talking with his traveling companions. He walked over to where I was sitting and hugged me as he asked me who I was. It was clear to me that he was stoned; his navy eyes glazed and blurry, his movements as if in slow motion, his inhibitions misplaced.

"I'm the pastor here at the church," I said, and everyone laughed. "Your name?"

"One Gallon."

"How'd you get that name?"

"I carried a gallon of water from Virginia to Maryland."

Later, One Gallon found me sitting outside and sat next to me to talk.

"My friend's in the hospital from a drug overdose," he said. "I'm in recovery too. I kind of lost hope when he overdosed. He was doing so well. You have to know this guy—he's so charismatic, such a good and fun guy. I looked up to him; it's like he pulled me down with him."

"I'm sorry, One Gallon. I know this must be hard on you."

"I've struggled to stay clean, been smoking on the trail and drinking too, but staying away from the hard stuff."

"Kind of difficult to stay away from the hard stuff when you are doing the soft stuff, isn't it?"

"Yeah." He looked down.

"My daughter has struggled with addiction," I said. "I don't think a person is ever entirely free of it; it finds its way in, but never completely out, no matter how long a person stays away from it. I've never seen anything destroy a life like drug addiction, nor anything as fast."

"I know. I've disappointed my parents. I was making a lot of money as an electrician, and I spent it on drugs. I'm trying to stay in recovery while on the trail. Thought it would be easier than being out there, but it's not. There're lots of drugs, easy to find, on and off the trail."

"I guess it comes down to deciding what life you want. You get to choose, and everyone else has to live with your decisions. Your friend is thirty years old and may be on dialysis for the rest of his life. His family will pay the bills or the government, and he will no longer have the same freedoms he had yesterday, probably ever again. You know, I've been thinking a lot about my own life, how I can't shift into reverse. You don't know how many times I wish I could, but none of us can."

There was something about One Gallon—a sensitivity, perhaps, or maybe it was that he just seemed like a soft place for others to fall;

perhaps that was because he had hit rock bottom at least once in his life. He knew how hard the ground was and how cold.

"I don't want to go back to New England where I'm from. I want to move out west and be a ski bum in Wyoming."

"There's something about you, One Gallon. I don't know exactly what it is or how to explain it, but there's something. Being a ski bum sounds like fun for a time. I don't know if you suffer as some do from a fear of growing up, or settling down, or whatever, but whatever it is, I pray you will stare it in the face. Confront it. I know of little else that is as heartbreaking and destructive as drug addiction. I hope that your friend's overdose will help you run for your life, not away from it."

A fellow hiker came for him then, urging him to join the group for a few drinks and food at a bar across the street that locals claim is haunted. A previous owner had been murdered there, and earlier, the restaurant had fallen victim to an arsonist that had never been identified.

One Gallon hesitated, then stood up and bent over to hug me good-bye. I didn't see him after that.

The next morning I drove Twirl to the hospital with her gear.

"I'm going to say goodbye to Rocky and his parents, and then I'm going to get back on the trail. The others are going to wait for me. I can't leave Rocky and then be alone."

"I understand," I said, and we embraced.

Watching her lace the straps over her back and move under the weight of her pack toward the hospital entrance, I felt as if I was saying goodbye to my child, the same way I felt when I bid One Gallon goodbye. True what I said about choices when I was with them, but there is one choice that remains true no matter how many times it's denied. We are connected by some cosmic web that shimmers in the morning light and seems invisible in the darkness but is unbreakable no matter how many times it unravels or frays. We are each other's keepers, even as we let each other go.

INJURED

... but from the tree of the knowledge of good and evil
you shall not eat, for in the day that you eat from it you
will surely die.

Genesis 2:17
New King James Version

H *OW FAR DOWN DOES GRACE go?*
    During a unit of Clinical Pastoral Education, I learned about moral injury, a wound that requires grace in small doses to heal; it cannot take grace all in at once.

From my first encounter with Arnie, it was clear to me that he had suffered a fall in life and struggled to rise ever since. I didn't know the details, or how far he had fallen, until close to his death, when he was in his early eighties. He told me why he was on Meagan's List and the circumstances around his going to prison. He never told me whether what he had done to his victim had been done to him or not. He told me that when he was baptized, all that clung to him was washed away.

Arnie had heavy-lidded eyes as if half-shut against the world, as if he only saw half of it. He was partially bald but still had vestiges of auburn hair and long sideburns. His spine had a slight bend to it, almost like a crease, so he was always leaning a bit forward, making him appear shorter than his six-foot-three frame. He suffered a stutter; he'd catch syllables with his breath and relax his tongue around the words that would eventually come out, all windy and flimsy; his breathing was labored, emphysemic, and audible. His clothes often smelled of oil and diesel, like a mechanic's, and he had large hands with long fingers and shiny, smooth fingernails that were curved downward, almost claw-like.

Hikers appreciated Arnie showing up at the center on any given day to shuttle them around town in return for a small donation. Unless, of course, they didn't pay, and then Arnie would get angry and fly into the center, screaming at whomever he felt had taken advantage of him. He plastered his car with vinyl lettering on his car's hatchback door condemning abortion, with "Arnie's Shuttle Service" pasted on the hood.

One day, an angry male hiker approached David inside the center, livid about Arnie's sexually suggestive comments to a young woman whose trail name was Chilly. Arnie had given them a ride to Walmart the day before. David reassured the hiker, who was in his early thirties (and to whom I would have given the trail name Rage, given the opportunity), that he would speak to Arnie about it. Rage was medium height, wore glasses, his dark hair short and trimmed. He reminded me of a hot-headed actuary. I expected him to yank out a calculator from his shirt pocket at any moment to add up all of Arnie's offenses and deficits.

When Arnie pulled up in his car and got out, Rage charged at him.

"You owe Chilly an apology, you old man," Rage said, in a raised voice, his face up in Arnie's face.

Arnie swore back at him and yelled, "You had me running all over town, and you gave me nothing but a dollar." He called Rage something I couldn't repeat.

David, standing next to them, told Rage to back off. Arnie then grabbed Rage by the throat and started choking him. I was standing about twenty feet away when I looked up to witness what was happening. David began to yell at them, then pushed his way between them, breaking Arnie's stranglehold.

"Arnie, you're out of here. Leave, leave now!" David shouted, then turned to the hiker and told him he too had to leave, to pack up his stuff and get out.

After some more words, Arnie got into his car and flew down the driveway. The hiker continued to argue with David.

"I told you I would confront Arnie. You never go after someone like that in front of others—I told you I'd take care of it."

"He's a perverted old man," Rage said. "He owes Chilly an apology."

David continued to insist he would have confronted Arnie had Rage given him the chance. "He's done. He won't be shuttling hikers anymore."

"Then why do I have to leave?" Rage said, up in David's face.

I left the two of them to argue it out and went to find Chilly. She sat crying at the picnic table out in front of the center, burying her head in her hands.

I sat next to her and put my arm around her shoulders. "It's okay," I said. "I know you're upset. What just happened is upsetting."

"I didn't mean for that to happen," she said. She told me she was eighteen. She had finished high school that summer and had been hiking since early July. She had met Rage several hundred miles back, and he had acted as her protector.

She continued to sob. Her thin t-shirt hid little.

"I don't want him to have to leave; it's all my fault. I shouldn't have said anything."

"No, you should have, or how might this have ended? If you said nothing, then maybe the next young woman would have felt victimized by inappropriate things Arnie would've said. Can you tell me what some of those things were?"

"He said, if I were chilly, that he would take me home and warm me up, stuff like that."

"I'm sorry, truly I am. We'll see to it that he no longer drives hikers around."

"I don't want it to be because of me."

"Why not you?" I asked. "Do you think you're the only one he's done it to—or will do it to? He may have been saying stuff all along, and no one told us. Come on, let's go to my office. David will work this out with your friend."

After some heated discussion, David agreed to let Rage stay until the next day to hike out with Chilly since it was already midday, and they were waiting on a resupply box to arrive at the post office. Later that afternoon, Arnie called and left a message on my cell phone, crying and apologizing, "I don't know what got into me."

The following Sunday, Arnie slipped me a note, again with an apology.

"I don't know what got into me," he repeated.

I wanted to say, or what has never left you.

Arnie was forbidden to shuttle hikers from that day on. That winter, he made a trip to the Philippines to meet a woman he had met over the internet, whom he thought would care for him the rest of his days. When he arrived in Manila, he wasn't allowed to leave the airport due to the recent international sex offender reporting. The authorities forced him to return home without seeing her or meeting her in the flesh for the first time.

Within months, Arnie lay dying. He told me he was afraid to die. He made his confessions, he asked forgiveness of the girl, who was now a woman, that he had victimized. When I visited him the last time, he yelled out, "But I didn't penetrate her."

Of this I know, having sat at the bedside of many a-dying: *We die as we have lived.*

NOTES ALONG THE WAY

Distance hiking forces you to function in your most exposed, vulnerable state.

Sarah Kaizar

I N MY OFFICE, A BOX overflows with hiker journals that date back forty-plus years. Flipping through and reading a number of them, it's clear no one wants to forget the details of such an adventure or their travel companions.

The journals are records of moments and snapshots of trail life. They memorialize gains and losses; they keep conversations. Entries also tell others where to go in Delaware Water Gap and how far ahead they might be from others who might want to catch up.

Some hikers keep a personal journal of their 2,200-mile trek and track their miles per day, rooting themselves in time and writing a history of one's inner life. They will pass them down to children or future children or grandchildren, or friends, or just as living proof that once upon a time they broke free of their ordinary lives to venture into the wild, carrying little. Such a daring act deserves documentation.

But more, I am convinced that words, all words, have a life all their own. They are alive when they are spoken, sang, or written; they breathe, pant, gasp, make visible what is invisible, and live forever, even after silence rushes in their wake and displaces them. They make art out of one's life, as do the sketches and photographs. Somehow, words hide away in our spines and nerve endings, ready to erupt at any time.

Reading through these old journals, I witnessed epiphanies that brought a new way of seeing the world and others, a clarity, a flash of light in the dark, as if something rose up in them from within and they could look inside themselves. Sometimes entries read like a holy or unholy correspondence; the alphabetic characters like the foil of stained-glass windows.

Wednesday, January 2, 2002. Two years ago on this date my father died at Jackson Memorial Hospital in Miami. Cesar and I had just finished a year-long road trip to all 50 states (our honeymoon) and my parents were in town to welcome us home. They were in a car accident before we got there and my dad died from internal injuries. I did get to spend time with him before he died. At the time I thought I was being punished for following a preposterous dream. And part of me wonders what/ who the casualty will be this time, as I chase another dream--hiking from Maine to Georgia. Why do I have the privilege to live my dreams? And what is the cost? Only a human would dare to challenge the divine plan by thinking she and her mortal concerns affect things that are beyond reckoning--like death. But to admit that death is random would be to acknowledge my powerlessness in the end, though, that's what my hike is about: relinquishing my need to control people/things/ outcomes. Let go, and let God. I'm six months into it, with six yet to go. My New Year's Resolution is to be nicer to Cesar because he is my love and my life, and who knows the number of our days? Maud of "Cesar & Maud"

NO ROOM

While they were there, the days were completed for her to give birth. And she gave birth to her firstborn son; and she wrapped Him in cloths, and laid Him in a manger, because there was no room for them in the inn.

Luke 2:6-7
New American Standard Bible

DECEMBER DARK, THE AIR WAS luminous, the streetlights aglow. It would be a long night. Having just finished feeding my extended family on Christmas Eve afternoon, I was on my way to church for the seven o'clock Family Service. At ten o'clock, local jazz musicians would gather in the sanctuary to sing carols and tell stories until nearly midnight.

My cell phone rang. A young man's voice asked, "I wanted to know if I could stay at the hostel tonight. I called another number before, but the person hung up on me."

"Are you a hiker?"

"No. I've been living on the road for a few years now," he said.

"Where are you from?"

"New Jersey."

"Is there any way your family could come and get you tonight, being that it's Christmas Eve?" I asked.

"No, I can't go back home again. I haven't seen my family in five years."

It was bitter outside. I imagined the young man was thin, hungry, with hollow eyes, scruffy, with mossy teeth and dirty fingernails, carrying a worn pack, hands trembling in frayed gloves, his thumb in the air as he hitchhiked. He probably had layers of clothes on, but none thick enough to keep him warm. I thought I heard a slight shiver in his voice. I assumed a few things—that he may have been an addict or that he suffered some mental illness, or that his family was fractured for one reason or another, and it was too risky to go home again.

"I'm so, so sorry, Mike. We have a strict policy that our center is only for thru-hikers or section-hikers on the Appalachian Trail. I so want to say yes, but I can't go against what we have to be pretty strict about."

"I understand," he said, his voice more distant.

"Can you tell me about why you've been on the road for so long?"

"It's a long story."

"I have time," I said, wanting to at least give him "room" in my life.

"I didn't get along with my father, and I left when I turned eighteen."

"Where did you go? What did you do?"

"Stayed with friends, hitchhiked around the country, did odd jobs."

"Do you want to go home again?"

"I can't."

"I'm sorry, it's the mother in me, the pastor in me. I don't mean to simplify your history or to be naive. I know sometimes the chasm grows deeper and wider the longer we stay away. I don't know what transpired in your family. It's Christmas Eve, and I want so much to give you shelter tonight, and I feel like a complete hypocrite that I can't."

"I understand," he said.

We spoke for a few more minutes, and then he said goodbye.

I went into the church, knowing we hadn't offered sanctuary to a road-weary, wounded traveler who had no destination in mind. Couldn't we have made an exception?

The memory of the attack and the shooting of the homeless man in the center two decades earlier had never faded; the "hikers only" policy was in place for good reason. I knew that. But there was a nagging ache inside me for this son.

* * *

Months earlier, another man in his twenties, heavy-set, with crud on his teeth, had wandered into the center in late August. He had slept outside at night; he wasn't a thru-hiker—you can always tell by the clothes one wears and the gear one carries. He slipped in during the early shadows of the evening as if he wouldn't be noticed and bunked down on a spot of unoccupied grass, his black dog beside him. The next morning one of the men who helped out at the center told him he had to move on, so he gathered all the belongings he had in the world, stuffed them into his pack, and headed down to the nearby Visitor's Center. From there, he called me.

"I need to get to upstate New York where my father lives," he said.

I don't usually drive with men or strangers alone in my car—it's part of the clergy sexual misconduct policy I abide by. I offered him a bus ticket when he informed me he had a dog and could not ride the bus.

"How have you been traveling?"

"Hitchhiking, walking."

I didn't know anyone who could or would take him eighty miles north.

"By the way, how did you end up at the church last night?"

"A state trooper dropped me off."

It sometimes happened that law enforcers—state troopers, federal rangers, local police—would drop wanderers off at the Hikers Center.

"Let me call you back." I hung up and called a local taxi service who agreed to take a man and his dog on the trip for a hundred and twenty dollars.

I called the young man back and agreed to meet him at the Visitor's Center, where I would give the taxi driver the cash.

It wasn't hard to spot him, a ragged young man in torn jeans, who appeared to be more than one shower short, with the pit bull at his side. He walked toward me with open arms as if we were old friends meeting up; his large long arms wove themselves around me.

* * *

There was a moment in my life when I was homeless in the sense that I had no shelter to call my own. I was twenty-two, married, and had a five-month-old infant in the back seat of an orange Chevy Chevette. Everything we had was either shoved into the compact car or had been crowded into a friend's garage for storage. My husband and I drove down to the end of the quarter-mile driveway and stopped. We prayed, "Lord, which direction do we turn?"

Our commitment ended to restore a country estate home owned by a wealthy family in affluent Westchester County, New York. We had committed to working eight hours a week each in exchange for rent, along with another newlywed couple. The home had been abandoned over a decade earlier. It was once an elegant mansion that sat high on a hill with a wide veranda wrapped around the front and sides of the house. Every room had a fireplace, except the kitchen. Movie stars and Hollywood notables from the 1940s had spent many a day here.

One Christmas, we hosted over sixty friends for a sit-down dinner in the dining room. But the house had been neglected for a long time, and even after a year and a half and over twelve thousand hours of labor, there was still plenty of work to do. I learned how to spackle and sand, torch alligatored exterior paint off the clapboard without burning the house down, and other renovation skills while living there.

A few months before we were to move, my father drove up from New Jersey for the day to help me with my hours as I was caring for my newborn, my father's first grandchild. He arrived on a damp and chilly Saturday morning in October with tools in hand. We worked alongside each other outside, torching and scraping scaled paint off the clapboard siding as I carried my daughter on my back. We talked about many things, but never of the one thing I had always wanted to talk about, the one thing I learned was too unsafe to discuss, simply put, *What the hell happened nine years ago and ever since?* But there was something healing in that he had driven over an hour just to be with my child and me, to help out.

"What are you going to do when your commitment is up here?" Dad asked.

"Not sure yet. We've got a couple of months."

Behind him was the woods with trees in mid-turn, golden at the edges, scarlet too, but blazing against the canvas of low clouds.

"I have a cottage on a small lake in Jersey. If you need a place to stay for a while, you can stay there."

I imploded then. I dared not show it. Something like a bone lodged in my throat. Was this the long-awaited invitation into his life?

The next afternoon after church, my husband, infant, and I piled into the Chevette and traveled to the private and hidden lake community in Stockholm, about an hour and a half drive away. It was rainy and cold. Since it was autumn, the lake houses were closed and vacant for the season. A dirt road encircled the lake, and we followed it to the left, about halfway around when I saw the sign, *Blackbeard's Island*. At first, I smiled at my father's inherent playfulness, but I also felt robbed of him over the past nine years. Had he suffered as we had? Had he just got on with his new life and never looked back?

We parked the car near the edge of the road and walked down a narrow pathway to a wooden footbridge. We crossed over onto the island, into his life, into an unshared history. I held my infant daughter close to me, the way I imagined my father had once held me as if I could protect her from what felt like would be an awful revelation. We saw the brown, rough clapboard cottage amid the trees, facing away from us from the other side of the bridge. Then, I saw a clothesline. Hanging from it, stiff and shuddering in the chilly wind, was a little girl's bathing suit, faded red and well worn. Beneath it was riding toys and a sandbox soggy with rain.

"A young child?" I don't remember if I said the words out loud or not. "The woman he's with has a young child?" By the size of the bathing suit, the child had to be no older than five. I realized then the child had to be his.

We walked around to the front of the cottage. In a kind of stunned silence, I climbed up the stairs to the screened porch, where we found the key that had been stashed away. Inside was rustic and basic. It had the scent of a cabin—musty and damp.

The kitchen was small with a few pine cupboards, a stainless steel sink, and only a few feet of counter space. Behind the kitchen was a small bunk room where my father's daughter must have slept, unaware that she had four half-siblings in the world who knew nothing of her. We had to walk through the living room to get to the bedroom on the far side of the cabin. I stared at the double bed in the room, then at the open closet where my father's clothes hung alongside a woman's. Some medicine bottles were on the dresser with the name Mary on them.

The next afternoon my father called.
"You have a daughter, Dad?"
"Yes," he said.
"What's her name?"
"Diane."
"You're married?"
"Yes, I thought you knew that."
"How could I, when you never told any of us, not even mom?"

* * *

"Lord, which way do we turn?" we asked, three months later.

It was January. We had nowhere to go. Too cold to go to my father's cabin. We turned right and headed toward a friend's house, who offered us an open invitation to stay with them for as long as we needed. Sam and Vicki were in their late forties with three teenage children. When we arrived at their modest ranch house, their sons carried our suitcases and portable crib into the master bedroom. No matter how much we objected, they insisted on giving us their shimmering white and silver bedroom, while Sam and Vicki were emphatic about sleeping on the living room floor, night after night, for a month.

"Vicki, Sam," I said, "I can't stay at your house and have you sleep on the floor. I can't do it."

"Sherry, if Jesus were coming to your house, where would you put Him?"

"But I'm not Jesus, Vicki. Please let us be the ones sleeping on the floor."

She asked me again, "If Jesus were coming to your house, where would you put Him?"

She'd pause and then answer her question as if there could only be one answer: "You would put him in the best room in the house."

For the next thirty days, she swore it was the best thing that ever happened to her back.

* * *

I was granted shelter, a home not of my own, a place to lay my head at night, a kitchen to prepare my meals, a safe place to nurse my baby. It was a different kind of homelessness. In the months that followed, we would move into an apartment and move out again two months later due to the astronomical cost of heating the apartment over a five-car garage. We then moved in with my in-laws for a month. By June, we packed the car one more time and traveled away from our friends and faith community to my father's lake house, into the periphery of his life, sleeping in the same bed he had shared with the "other" woman.

Over time I came to understand that one can be emotionally homeless even when he or she has a place to call one's own. Home is where you inhabit the shared space of those who you love and who love you back. I had years of feeling terribly alone in the world after my father left—he had been, after all, my first home.

That's what rushed back at me that Christmas Eve—that inner vacancy of being left in the world when I told the young man there was no room at the church for him to lay his head for the night. If we could have said yes, he would have heard Christmas carols being sung through the old floorboards of the church; he would have heard the story of the woman who had been turned away by an Innkeeper for there was no room, no vacancy, even though she was about to give birth. He could have listened to the story of a homeless man whom some called the Son of God.

OUT OF THE WOODS

Those who contemplate the beauty of the earth find reserves of strength that will endure as long as life lasts.

Rachel Carlson

THE TRAIL IS A PLACE where some people find a way to resurrect without dying first. They go into the forest, more than one hiker confessed to me, to find their way out of the woods. Hiking was an alternative to suicide.

Palm Sunday, 2016, a Federal Park Ranger dropped a brother and sister off at the church, then called me. He had found them camping in a forbidden area of the Delaware Water Gap National Recreation Area. He ran their identifications to see if they were wanted by the law and, finding they weren't, brought them to the center for shelter. It turns out, no one wanted them and no one was searching for them. All they had was each other. In their twenties, both were biracial, with hair dyed platinum, tall and thin, wearing dark jeans and jackets. They carried school-size backpacks. The woman wouldn't look me in the eye when I asked them their names.

"Lucia," she said.

"Jake," he said.

"Where are you from?"

"Upstate New York."

"The ranger tells me you are hiking the trail?" He also told me that they had no money. I handed them all the money I had on me, about forty dollars, enough to eat for a few days.

"Yes, we're trying to get to Arkansas."

"Are you running away?"

"No, just leaving behind an abusive home." They shared how there were all kinds of physical and drug abuse and that they had to flee to find something to live for. I asked if they were warm enough, as the nights were cold and their clothes looked insufficient for living on the trail.

"We've got layers on underneath," Lucia said.

They were polite and respectful but appeared almost paralyzed while talking to me. Having hitchhiked and camped and hiked over the last two weeks, they had covered a hundred miles. They stayed at the center for the night. A week later, they would return to the church as they had wandered without a map and circled back unintentionally. They stayed for another night, after which I never saw them again.

A week later, Easter Sunday, I woke at five in the morning to shower, dress, gulp down a cup of coffee, and dress in layers before heading to the trail to hold a sunrise service at six-thirty. It was still dark, around thirty-eight degrees, and misty when I arrived at the Gap trailhead. I hiked a tenth of a mile to the edge of Lake Lenape. The water had breached its boundary and now flowed down the hillside due to rain and beaver dams. A hiker named Follower was already there, an older guy with a soiled blue parka. His beard looked a week or two old, all barbed. I recognized him as someone who had stayed at the center the night before. He'd been hiking for a few weeks and was giving himself a year to do the entire AT.

There wasn't much time to talk with him as others were arriving for the service. About twenty in all straggled through the woods, sleep still on their faces, a dull glaze in their eyes, and fat coats around them as they folded their bodies against the bitter wind. Before and during the service, there was much looking up into the sky, waiting for the sun's first streaks. Deep breathing, too, as if they were inhaling the trees that scrubbed the inside of their lungs. Like me, they wanted their clothes to smell like rain by the time we left the woods. Minted, fresh, aired out.

We sang, and we recalled that morning two thousand years ago when the tomb was found empty. I knew that we had all come for the revelation of that discovery, for that inner thunder and high-voltage lightning that rolls stones away from our tombs of weariness, power-lessness, darkness, and casts off whatever crown of thorns we wear.

On this particular Easter morning, it was impossible not to think about death since suicide had become an epidemic that spring in our area. Between January and March, three local teens—a sixth-grader, a freshman, and a junior in high school—killed themselves, two by hanging, one by gunshot. Another twenty-year-old man two days be-fore confessed to one of the college professors who attends the church that he had tried to commit suicide to prove that he hadn't been stalk-ing a female student on campus.

I spoke of the women who went to the tomb to anoint Jesus's body with burial spices but found life instead of death. After the service, Follower said, "I am a disciple of Yeshua. I stayed at the hostel in 1979 on my attempted NOBO thru-hike," he said. "The Lord is risen indeed. It is a joy to know the forgiveness of sins and share in the everlasting life of the resurrection." His face was full of sun now that the sun had penetrated the clouds; he didn't tarry for long, speaking briefly to a few others before heading up the steep stony path.

Back at the church, I passed the church's Memorial Garden planted near the base of the stairs that lead up to the sanctuary as if one has to pass through death before entering life. The garden was created in memory of a woman who had committed suicide years earlier. Easter lilies were forcing their way up through the hardened earth, as were hostas, but much of the garden was still barren and dark. In time, phlox, buttercups, and irises would bloom. One jolt of color—a turquoise-dyed hardboiled egg, leftover from an egg hunt the day before, was hidden in a wind-swept pile of dead leaves. As I climbed the stairs, I thought about the woman whose ashes were scattered there. Like too many, she had gone into the ground rather than into the woods to find her way out of dark thickets of despair.

RAIN

Open your mind to what I shall disclose, and hold it fast within you; he who hears, but does not hold what he has heard, learns nothing.

Dante Alighieri

M INDFUL PULLED A PLASTIC SANDWICH bag from his pack with a photograph inside. He cupped it in his left hand as if it was too valuable or delicate for anyone else to touch or to hold. It held him, I thought. It was a photo of his father, probably in his late twenties, sitting on a couch with his arms around his three sons, all appearing to be under the age of six. A broad smile lit the man's face. His left arm lapped over two sons on his left; his right arm held Mindful, who looked about three.

"My father committed suicide on Christmas Eve in 2003 when I was thirteen," Mindful said matter-of-factly. "And my brother on the other side of my father died when he was three of neuroblastoma, a rare pediatric cancer. I was just five when that happened."

"I'm truly sorry," I said, aching inside. I stared at the image of his father wearing blue jeans and a red golf shirt, sitting in front of a picture window. "I can only imagine how those losses have impacted your life."

At such moments I hated words; they are too small, too insignificant, little more than a dull knife to cut off a portion of another person's grief in hopes of lessening it by the mere presence of another human being. But silence is impossible to read, so words are spoken.

Mindful had a Freudian look about him. He wore frameless glasses, had dark curly hair, a fuzzy beard, a constant sweet half-smile, and a face thinner than his father's. There was a maturity about him that I assumed suffering had forced on his youth.

"He died from alcoholism; it killed him. I'm in recovery too, and I have bipolar disorder." Again, he spoke in such a matter-of-fact way as if the truth of who he was—where he came from, where he was going—was his air. He had to breathe it, or he'd suffocate. He slid the photograph back into the plastic bag and laid it on the table in front of him. "I wrote my college thesis on spirituality as a healing tool for mental illness and addiction. Before I was in recovery, I was an atheist."

"Being in recovery convinced you there's a God?" I asked.

"I witnessed firsthand, through others and my own experience, the power of spirituality. I decided to do my college thesis on spirituality as a healing modality. Initially, I was averse to spirituality because I thought it was closely related to organized religion. But I came to understand that spirituality was a much broader, all-encompassing concept."

"Organized religion gets a bad rap for good reasons," I said. "A fellow clergyman once said to me that he thought organized structures were demonic—I've never stopped thinking about that."

"I live by John Muir's quote, 'I would rather be in the mountains thinking about God than in a church thinking about the mountains,'" Mindful said.

"I love that quote too, but I think we need both cathedrals. It hasn't been easy, and it's not that easy to say, but I've come to believe that we can't truly know God without each other," I said. "We can only know what we know, share what we believe, and what we have experienced. I would like to hear more about your thesis."

"I collected interviews from those in recovery, from clergy, and medical professionals, and experienced for myself just how powerful spirituality is in the healing process when it comes to addiction and mental illness. It's a new field in medicine, and it's been neglected in part because it's an inexact science. You can't really define spirituality."

I remembered the day I discovered my oldest daughter, at seventeen, was addicted to heroin. I remembered the lies she told, the excuses she made, all the things and people she blamed, including me. I had become convinced ever since that once addiction is in the blood, it never leaves. It possesses. It roves, craves itself, thirsts, ravages, prowls, and roars.

"I quote Carl Jung in my thesis," he said, flicking through his cell phone to find the document. Then he read: "Jung wrote that he saw craving for alcohol in alcoholics as 'the equivalent, on a low level, of the spiritual thirst of our being for wholeness, expressed in medieval language: the union with God.'" He continued, "Both my father and my grandfather died of alcoholism. I thought I wanted to go to medical school to be a psychiatrist but decided against it because I don't want to be in a profession that is all about prescribing medications. I just love spiritual inquiry."

"Have you thought about divinity school?"

"I have. I've been thinking not about being a pastor but a spiritual counselor. I love people's stories. I'm not sure that there's only one pathway to God. When you posit that the revelation is sealed, there's a root of religious intolerance. What I know is that God works through people. I experience it all the time," he said.

The conversation ended there, upon his promise to email me his thesis. As I initially skimmed through it, I saw the dedication was "For Dad."

Two months later, I received a text and a photograph from Mindful on the last day of August. He was standing atop Mt. Katahdin, his arms outstretched in the air.

"Did it, Rev. Blackman! What an absolutely amazing journey! I'm so glad our paths crossed, and I will be in touch soon about divinity school plans. I really appreciate the words of encouragement you gave me when we met at the hostel. God bless and be well," he wrote.

His hands were open, full of the sky; a tiny edge of the photograph stuck out from his shirt pocket and glittered in the afternoon light.

A year later, Mindful reached out to me again as he was considering applying to seminary to pursue his vocational goal. He wanted advice since he wasn't tied to any faith community and had no affiliation with any church. He shared his application essay with me, much that had to do with his experience hiking the AT.

Here is what he wrote:

The first time I visited North Carolina was on foot. It was a cold, rainy day, but I was thrilled. I had just finished hiking through Georgia, the first state of the Appalachian Trail (AT), and made it to North Carolina. At that point, the journey was a physical one, but over the 2,189-mile course, it became a spiritual one.

For the three days leading up to that, I had been hiking with a man whose nickname was Turtle. I first encountered Turtle while he was eating a snack at the side of the trail, and I chose to stop hiking and start a conversation with him. We began hiking together, and we continued until he completed his planned section, just shy of the North Carolina border. He turned out to be a Disciples of Christ minister from Virginia, and much of what we spoke about while walking together—family, friendships and relationships, service to others, faith in God—was related to spirituality. That he was a Christian minister and that I had chosen to hike the AT as part of my own discernment process seemed more than just a coincidence.

On the trail, there were many challenges and setbacks—rain, cold, darkness, fatigue, blisters, and injury—much as there are in life. Usually, the challenges were short-lived, but not always. At one point, as it rained unrelentingly for four days straight, I thought of the family members I have lost. My younger brother Patrick died of neuroblastoma, a rare pediatric cancer, when he was three, and I was five. When I was 13 years old, on Christmas Eve 2003, my father committed suicide. The grieving processes after those tragedies were extended periods of rain for me, which in the moment I felt would never lift. But the memory of getting through those emotionally difficult times helped me keep faith that the rain would eventually pass and I would be able to complete my trek.

There were also some sections that I was more excited to get through than I was to hike them. After about 250 miles, Virginia started to seem monotonous. I still had another 280 miles to hike to get through it. But by consciously centering myself in the present day and the trail I was walking, I made steady progress. Pennsylvania was also tough, with long stretches of trail made of rocks that took a serious toll on my feet. But I learned to rest my feet throughout the day, appreciate the change of scenery, and relish the interesting people I met while hiking that difficult stretch.

Those situations reminded me of how I viewed some of my academic experiences in college and the post-baccalaureate premedical program. My major at Wesleyan was an interdisciplinary social sciences program, which provided a broad liberal arts education, but toward the end of the program did not excite me as much as studying religion and spirituality. However, had I not experienced that challenging program, I doubt I would have developed the skills needed to thoroughly research and write my senior honors thesis on a topic I hope to explore further at Wake Forest: the intersection of spirituality and mental health.

The post-baccalaureate program at Mt. Holyoke was challenging because I had never taken a college science class before and, two days after graduating Wesleyan, found myself in a general chemistry class. While I am glad I completed a core college science education in the program, I decided that my goal was not to become a psychiatrist but a minister so that I could focus more heavily on the role of spirituality in mental health treatment. I feel that I needed to experience those detours both to gain the academic skills that they fostered and to gain clarity on what I wanted to pursue.

Finally, the trail was full of unexpected encounters that led me into friendships and experiences I could not have imagined. I realized, as Unitarian Universalism's seventh principle emphasizes, just how much I was living in "the interdependent web of all existence of which we are a part." Had I not stopped to say hello to Turtle, I never would have had the conversations that contributed to my discernment. This happened four other times on the trail, all with Christian ministers—Baptist, Presbyterian, nondenominational, and Catholic—who independently encouraged me to pursue ministry. I preferred to hike with older hikers, as I enjoyed asking them about their lives and the lessons they had learned along the way. Some of the most memorable conversations I have had in my life took place along that trail, though I realized that reaching out to other people—asking questions and letting them be heard—can be done anywhere, not only on a long-distance wilderness trail

When I began researching divinity schools, Wake Forest School of Divinity stood out to me as an ideal fit. While reading the mission statement, I found myself nodding in agreement with the type of place the School of Divinity strives to be. As a Unitarian Universalist, I am strongly attracted to the ecumenical nature of the school, as well as the focus on "justice, reconciliation, and compassion" in ministry.

I hope to return to North Carolina this fall, this time with a back-pack ready to be filled with books about theology and ministry. I will carry with me resilience, determination, and open-mindedness to thrive as a divinity student at Wake Forest School of Divinity. But I will also be keeping the school's motto, *Pro Humanitate*, close at heart. I am drawn to ministry to engage more closely with humanity around me; to learn more about what helps individuals thrive spiritually, mentally, and physically in their lives; to listen to the challenges they are facing; and to support them in their life journeys through service and compassion. I would be deeply grateful for the opportunity to continue learning and seeking at Wake Forest School of Divinity.

Mindful was accepted into Wake Forest—the perfect name for a young man further awakened in the woods and on the trail. In his thesis, he had quoted Jung saying, "I could not say I believe. I know! I have had the experience of being gripped by something that is stronger than myself, something that people call God.'"

RIVER

Night climbs up to the mountain. Hunger
goes down to the river.

Pablo Neruda

N OT FAR FROM THE CHURCH, about a mile down River Road,
I watch five young men from a beach bathing in the Delaware
River. I wonder if they are section-hikers taking a break from the trail
on this brilliant afternoon. Their backs are like peeled fruit as the water washes over them. White-skinned, sun-stained, pink-necked, they
swim across the river, side-by-side. They pop up where the water is
shallow, then dunk into the darker waters under a late afternoon September sky. Patches of chest hair look like roots growing through pale
soil. They hoot and holler; their amplified, husky voices carry up and
down the waters.

They float and dive, swimming back and forth where the river widens. The Delaware Water Gap Bridge is not far away, standing above
the fast-moving rapids that flow beneath it. The unwelcome blare of
traffic ricochets against granite rocks. I doubt these men are aware of
the lives the Delaware swallows every year. Everyone thinks this is a
quiet waterway, but it rages beneath the surface, where the eye cannot
see. Every year the currents claim unwilling sacrifices of at least two
or three adults mostly since children are forced to wear life preservers.
Last summer, a man capsized a canoe he was paddling with his toddler
son and wife, both wearing lifesaving vests. He fell into the water, into
its depths, and never surfaced again.

The Delaware is called the lifeblood of the Mid-Atlantic, and sometimes after a rain, it looks like blood—reddish-brown—that climbs up the banks and threatens the homes built too near its shore. The waters of the Catskill Mountains, further north in New York State, flow down into the river that separates Pennsylvania from New Jersey at this section, and then toward the Atlantic Ocean.

I listen to the soft lapping sound the swimmers' arms make as they lift above the surface and trail back down; I close my eyes for a second and inhale the wind, fragrant with a campfire from Worthington State Park across from me, and the sweet scent of trees still determined to hold onto their leaves. Sawbellies flicker in the afternoon light as they leap and ripple the surface.

Over the summer, some thru-hikers will take a zero-day and rent a raft, kayak, or canoe to mosey down the river, eyeballing eagles soaring above it, and sometimes a bear at its edge, washing, fishing, or cooling itself. Young people jump off forbidden cliffs while families and friends picnic on several of the mid-river islands. Today, the lavender light slants toward October, and fewer hikers and visitors are venturing out onto or into the river. The trodden AT has begun to heal as it buries its half-crushed acorns. In the morning, a velvety cloud will hover over these waters. Stones will steam; silence will swell as the days progress, as the howl returns to the wildlife.

SHERPAS

*Wise man is a good Sherpa; he takes you
to the highest places!*

Mehmet Murat Ildan

H IS TRAIL NAME WAS TREE Trunk for his girth, I suspected. Sitting on his truck's tailgate, he struggled to inch on and lace up his hiking shoes. Minutes earlier, he had stepped into my office and asked if he could leave his vehicle in the church parking lot for the day, as he was going to hike a seven-mile section of the AT. He promised to pick up his truck by late afternoon. Tree Trunk was in his fifties at least, I surmised, and he didn't look to be in great health. In a fit of compassion, I conceded.

After he finished tying his boots, I saw him hovering over a list of shuttlers and heard him calling on his cell phone about getting a ride to Fox Gap and then walking back to Delaware Water Gap. I had stepped outside to show him where to leave his truck when he ended the call. He approached me, asking, "Would you pray with me? I start every day on the trail praying with someone if I can find a praying man or woman."

"Of course," I said.

He shared: "My fiancée just texted me that she's having second thoughts about getting married. We're supposed to be married in a couple of months. She's been taking care of her mother, who's dying, and she feels she can't leave her." He started to cry; his voice bled out and his face whitened before his cheeks blotched into a scarlet web. I motioned for him to sit down in one of the chairs outside Fellowship House.

"I don't know why she's having second thoughts," he continued. His blue eyes had a slight bulge to them, and they seemed to pale as he spoke. He had a receding hairline and a short untrimmed beard. "I can't believe this is happening. We've never lived close. She lives in Canton, and I live in Chicago. We travel back and forth on the weekends between our two homes. She's been texting me this for the last four days."

"I can see you love her very much," I said.

"We met at a friend's wedding. I was hiking the trail then and had taken time off for the celebration. I finally got up the courage to ask her if she'd join me on a hike. She didn't consider what I did as hiking; she said it was mountain climbing." He laughed; his face brightened. "She said she'd come out and visit me on the AT, and she did—three times! That was two years ago. When I was in Vermont, I broke my ankle— I've got diabetes, take shots. Bones break easier, I think. I ended up with the Twelve Tribes, a religious community in Vermont. Do you know about them?"

"Actually, I do," I replied. "I had a college friend who moved to the Rutland area to start that Christian community back in the seventies. I don't know much about them or what happened to him, other than it seemed cultist to me back then."

"They have a hostel that hikers can stay in. They ended up taking care of me while my ankle healed. They tried to recruit me. I shared with them how I had spent time in seminary studying for the priesthood. Made it through my first-year vows, but I left."

"You left seminary?" I asked.

"I liked women too much," he said, then chuckled. "The Catholic Church runs deep in my blood. I have a cousin who's a priest with the Legionnaire Order, an order that still does exorcisms. But the kill point for me and the church was when my mom died. I was twenty-eight. Because she was divorced, her body couldn't be in the sanctuary since the church was sacred ground. My father left my mother—why should she be punished?"

"I understand," I said.

"I lost a love for the church. My faith has broadened since I left seminary," he continued, telling me about his failed marriage and his son and daughter. "I still love my ex on some level, even after she made all kinds of false accusations against me. I don't unlove people. My son went to live with her a few years ago; he's twenty-one now, he's gained a lot of weight. If my son walked the trail with me, I would sell everything I had and be his Sherpa. I'd give him whatever he needs."

I pictured him carrying his son's pack up the trail, leaving his own pack behind.

"What do you think your son would gain if he walked the trail?" I asked.

"The world, the interior world, awareness, fitness. Your senses change out there. You can't smell yourself or other hikers, but you can smell deodorant on someone; you can smell bears and water moccasins. You start to understand that you're part of something greater; you are interconnected with everything. What he's doing to himself is disconnecting from who he really is. He's gained a hundred pounds since he moved in with his mother; he's not working, he's not living."

A car drove up the driveway and parked; I assumed it was his ride. I offered to pray with him before he left, as he had requested. I prayed for his breaking heart, for his appetite for God. I prayed that his interior life would be vast as the world that rubbed up against him. I prayed for his patience with his fiancée and compassion.

I did not see him when he returned later that day. Still, I continue to see him in others every day—all who are hankering for something more than their everyday lives offer them—not just a heightened sensory life, or the ability to smell wildlife or their own fear, but the courage, and the willingness, to carry another person.

SKIDMORE

What good is it for someone to gain the whole world,
yet forfeit their soul?

Mark 8:36
New International Version

May 2016

Skidmore, I called her. A twenty-eight-year-old who already had
more international immersions than people twice her age. She physically embodied the image of a surfer girl from California with long
blonde hair and blue eyes with a tall, slim, sun-tanned figure; she was
strong-minded and self-possessed. It turned out she graduated from
my alma mater, Skidmore College, so I felt as if we knew each other
somehow, although I'm not sure she shared that feeling.

She worked with the Peace Corps in Central America for two years
before working for a Non-Governmental Organization in Kenya, doing
research with a small team in Nairobi that focused on testing water
quality and water pipe networks in search of safe water. The project
had been funded by the World Bank and the Gates Foundation. She
epitomized the millennial generation's best, being well-educated and
using her privilege and power to invest in such environmental and
humanitarian work.

Her soft voice hardened with a critical tone as she spoke of her
experience in Africa: "The people would come up to you and ask for
the shoes off your feet. I've been to developing countries, but Africa
has a handout culture. I've been to Zambia and Rwanda, I've worked
with people in El Salvador; I don't think Africa is so much poorer, but

because we perceive them as such, we've given them so much more than other places. When they see white people, it's give me, give me, give me. In Latin America, people have far more pride."

She continued to unpack the resupply box she had retrieved from the post office next door, sorting through small plastic bags of dry goods and organizing them into different piles on the coffee table. She didn't seem too interested in engaging in conversation, or maybe she was distracted by the task at hand.

I had been to Kenya before and planned to return in the fall; I had seen the poverty of Kibera, a slum in the middle of Nairobi. I, too, had witnessed the total lack of sanitation, the garbage-strewn ditches, and the flying toilets that polluted the broken ground that thousands called home. Green rivers of sewage trickled through the slippery muddy streets and alleyways simmering in the heat as children ran among the trash where pigs and dogs scrounged for food. Stench exhaled from invisible mouths, making foreigners repulse, recoil, and retreat.

While there, I was warned not to walk alone among the crowds gathered in front of makeshift corrugated kiosks, as it was very likely that the terrorist group Al Shabaab would kidnap any American they could get their hands on for ransom. Even when driving through Kibera on deeply rutted roads, a man reached into our van and yanked a necklace off a woman in the front seat. It was an excursion through human hell.

"Everyone hustles. It's a get what you can, any way you can, as much as you can culture," she continued. "Corruption is a way of life there."

"It sounds like you grew up pretty comfortably. How did your parents bring you up to be so worldly-minded and courageous?"

She paused for a moment, looking to her left as if the answer was somewhere else in the room, and all she had to do was collect and organize it, then speak. "We traveled a lot, went on a lot of road trips. We moved a couple of times. I studied abroad while I was in high school; I had to get out of where I was. When I was fifteen, I moved to Ecuador as an exchange student. I'd have to say that traveling is the best education for understanding yourself, your culture, your religion. It's a way to see what we share universally and what we don't."

She spoke in a way that suggested she had traveled to places she didn't want to go to. "I imagine that serving in the Peace Corps and having the experiences you had in Africa could have been a bit overwhelming," I added.

Skidmore stopped fussing with her stuff and looked up at me. I had her attention. "After I left the Peace Corps, I had a lot to process; I ended up going to therapy. The counselor said I had PTSD after living under the poverty line in El Salvador. I had to talk through what I was dealing with. I had to learn to take what's important and not carry the whole world around. When I got back from there, I went to Stanford, and that just compounded it, you know, going from a developing country to one of the top-rated universities. I needed to get a master's degree in environmental science to do the work I wanted to do, and I couldn't deal with it all." She paused, then said, "I never want to be who I was before I had these experiences. Just like everyone else, I'm always becoming something or someone."

"You've had a good deal of adventure in your life. It seems like walking the AT isn't as climactic as it might be for others."

She flung her long mane behind her shoulders. "I wanted to prove to myself I could do it, but let me say, Pennsylvania rocks have done a good job of testing my grit; you've got to have a certain amount of mettle to do it. As soon as it rained, I wanted to quit, but I've come to realize that bad days are okay. When I was in foreign countries, I wanted to throw in the towel many times, but I wanted more to finish what I started."

"What do you want to do when you complete the trail?"

"I've already started an environmental inn in California with some partners. It'll have twenty units, using alternative building containers, solar systems, truck containers. It'll primarily be a hostel with yurts and tiny luxury homes," she said as she resumed packing her backpack. "One thing I've learned walking the trail is that stuff is just too much of a burden; it weighs too much, you can't carry it all." She stood up and placed a blanket in the hiker's box, free for the taking. "Stuff is just a burden."

"Yes," I said, "the world is heavy enough."

SMILEY AND MEEKNESS

I grew up in this town, my poetry was born between the hill and the river, it took its voice from the rain, and like the timber, it steeped itself in the forests. Green was the silence, wet was the light, the month of June trembled like a butterfly.

Pablo Neruda

S MILEY AND MEEKNESS, BOTH SIXTY-SEVEN years old, arrived together and introduced themselves to me when I stepped into the center in early May. Smiley was bent at the waist, struggling with a severe limp. She had a wide smile with a mouthful of white teeth, cropped steel-colored hair, and amber eyes. Meekness was quick to inform me that they were not a couple and that he had been helping Smiley since she was injured. It was her second knee injury while hiking; last year, she had shattered her ankle and had to abandon the trail.

Swinging her bangs to the side as she spoke, she said, "I don't want to get off the trail. I want to keep hiking. I have to be out here."

I told her we had a physical therapist in the church I would contact, ask to stop in, and check out her injury.

Meekness, a thin man with a profound Southern accent, soft gray eyes, a sparse whitening beard, and frameless glasses, said they had been hiking together for a while. They had met last year, and this year their paths intersected again only minutes before he would have missed her entirely; she was coming toward a shelter as he was just about to leave, hundreds of miles back.

"It was no accident. I knew when I saw her, I was to walk alongside her. We talk about God all the time."

I offered Smiley crutches that were kept at the center to keep weight off her injured leg. A short time later, we sat together at a favorite local eatery, The Village Farmer, a New England-style country market with every kind of homemade pie—raspberry, blueberry, cherry, apple, you name it. As Meekness and Smiley each wolfed down a chicken pot pie, a hot dog, and apple pie, they shared their stories.

Smiley went first. "I have been back in America for only three years. Before that, I was in Indonesia, serving with the Peace Corps teaching English," she said. "I had to learn Arabic, wore a headscarf, stayed with a Muslim family. When I came back, I moved in with my son in Arizona. Everything I have I can hold in my car. I don't want stuff. I don't want anything. I want to be out here, on the trail, in nature. This is where I am most myself."

She said that she had one prayer—to find the love of her life—and then she was quick to say what a great guy Meekness was, but he was married. Meekness jumped in and reassured me that he was happily married and that his wife wasn't all that crazy about the amount of time he had been spending with Smiley, often having to share sleeping quarters, and once in a while, a motel room.

I thought about Smiley's one prayer and her age, how the longing for love had never died despite two marriages, two children, and two divorces. Up until the time she joined the Peace Corps in her late fifties, she said she had done various jobs, but nothing really stuck until then, but hiking, being outdoors, and praying for love did.

In that split second, I recalled a quote that I had found while rifling through a file buried in a box at the Hikers Center, discovered a few months earlier. It was dated January 20, 1983, typed on a piece of paper that also had a copy of an article written by David Douglas about preserving the wilderness because of what it holds for us spiritually.

The quote was from Pablo Neruda's *Memoirs*: "My world expanded upward and outward along the towering trails . . . that communion, that revelation, that pact with the wilderness is still part of my life."

I saw in Smiley that same pact she had made knowingly or unknowingly. She had fused with the wilderness as if her blood was now a chemical concoction of elements—iron and river, copper and stone, and she could never leave this immersive communion, at least not without leaving something of herself behind. In the wilderness, primal longings emerge with new force.

In the article by Douglas below Neruda's quote, he wrote from old "Federalist Papers" of the wilderness movement. One phrase kept catching my eye, not only for how frequently it was expressed by the participants but also for how seldom it is heard today: "the need to preserve wilderness for its spiritual values." Few speakers bothered to define what these "spiritual values" were. They took it for granted that the audience—having sojourned in deserts, mountains, and forests—knew firsthand what was meant. It was the silence and solitude afforded by backcountry, the sense of awe it inspired, the way it could alter a traveler's soul as much as his sinews.

Meekness followed after Smiley. "My middle name is Meechan, so I thought—I'll be Meekness on the trail. I grew up during the Vietnam War, but I couldn't serve due to a knee problem. When I was fifty-five, everything changed. I went on a mission trip to Vietnam after being invited by a Vietnamese pastor of an underground church. The first day I got there, I just wanted to go home, and I told the group leader that. Our contact for the underground church wasn't allowed in the country, so we were on our own, and we just did prayer walks. I went back for five years. Faith took time to stick to me or me to it."

He explained that he had attended a revival meeting down in Kentucky when he was twelve years old, where he's from. When the evangelist had an altar call, "I prayed, Lord, if you want me to go down, then get me up—I prayed that—and I was halfway down the aisle, and I hadn't moved—I am not kidding you. But it wasn't until I went on those mission trips that my whole life changed."

I asked him what it was that changed him.

"I'm not sure I can say, maybe it was serving others, losing myself, sort of like Smiley talks about being in the wilderness, being part of the larger human family, not just my own. I think it was allowing myself to be caught by the Spirit, as strange as that may sound."

Meekness continued, telling us how he had built a company of his own and later sold it, only to be "let go" by the same company a few years later.

"By that time, I was near retirement age," he said. "I was asked to be involved with a medical mission to Haiti coordinating medical supplies, and I've been doing it ever since. Been to Haiti about fifty times. I've never been more at peace or happier in my life."

As these two retirement-aged individuals continued to talk, I couldn't help but compare them, how one was still looking for love, and the other seemed to have found it for his own life. Meekness had a wife and appeared content enough, although he offered he might have to leave Smiley behind due to pressure from his wife and continue his walk alone.

Smiley confided that she wasn't attracted to Christianity, at least not the brand Meekness was living. She had lived in an Islamic country; Muslim rituals and faith had grown thin roots in her, but not enough to convert to Islam. Buddhist practices had attracted her too. She was undecided, standing mid-stream at a confluence of religions, and she was grateful to have Meekness as a hiking companion, figuring God was on his side, so maybe hers too.

That evening, Sandy, our resident physical therapist, came and evaluated Smiley and set her up with bandages and an apparatus so that she wouldn't have to abandon her hike. Within a few days, she was standing almost straight. Meekness hiked out two days before Smiley did, under his wife's orders.

Smiley's prayer left me questioning: How many others were wandering on the trail, not counting steps or days or months, but praying to stumble upon the one thing they were looking for, the rock to build their life upon, or the love of their life, as in Smiley's case? And, how many "wander" through their days waiting for something or someone to fill an emptiness? How many are waiting for that one thing, but it never seems to come?

What if all that fluttering within us is evidence that it's all right here, right now, but we can't see "the forest for the trees?"

THE FALL OF OUR DISCONTENT

God has mercifully ordered that the human brain works slowly; first the blow, hours afterwards the bruise.

Walter de la Mare

THE SUMMER OF 2017 WEIGHED heavy with rain and humidity. Its gravity bore down upon us, leaving us short-tempered. By early September, the air thinned; the heat began to evaporate, leaving the ground parched and thirsty. Water sources dried up on the AT. South-bound hikers, mixed with a few straggling northbounders—who would have to flip-flop to summit Mt. Katahdin before the snows—came and went from the center searching for water and shelter.

Early Labor Day, I received a call about an altercation between a neighbor and a hiker in the middle of the night. The state police were called. I didn't know the neighbor, Lena, well; the older woman who had lived there for a long time had died the year before. I was told her husband, Sean, suffered post-traumatic stress disorder after several deployments in Iraq and Afghanistan.

According to Lena, a hiker had called the police after Sean had fired an air-soft pistol into a woodpile to scare away an animal. The hiker, camped out near the neighbor's property line, claimed that Sean had been threatening and intimidating, shooting the pistol near her tent. When the state police arrived without their strobe lights on, Sean came out of his house with the gun. He and Lena were both thrown to the ground, then handcuffed. Sean later admitted he thought it was a hiker coming to the door.

I asked Lena if she and Sean would meet with David and me at the church to discuss what had happened. She agreed. I heard Sean yell in the background, "This is going to end today!"

By the time I arrived at the church an hour later, David was already there, as was his wife, Bonnie. Five minutes later, Lena and Sean were walking up the driveway. I stood at the door, holding it open, with my arm outstretched to greet them. Sean looked at my hand as if it was a weapon, but then he shook it, keeping his elbow pressed close to his side. His movements were stiff, his lips tight. His eyes interrogated me. I felt guilty of something but not sure what.

The four of us sat around the table just inside Fellowship House. Sun streamed through the large windows behind the table and alongside it, but the light and warmth felt out of place, seemed to break apart, shatter when it fell upon us. The sting of alcohol was in the air.

I studied Sean as he sat spine-straight. He had blond hair and a pale complexion; his eyes were a hard blue, like glacier ice. He had the hands of a working man, muscular, with small gashes on his fingertips.

"This is going to end today," he said again. "I've tolerated enough. I'm going to the town and shutting the Hikers Ministry down." His hands curled into fists. I expected him to smash them against the table.

I saw David grow rigid in the chair. "You can't do that. We've been doing this for forty-one years. You've lived here, what, six months?"

Testosterone saturated the atmosphere. It was like watching two dogs bare their teeth with their fur standing up, circling each other. Lena, Bonnie, and I were like their masters trying to hold them back with invisible leashes.

Lena, who sat directly across from me, was silent and looked scared. She appeared tired and weary from a sleepless night, likely traumatized by the incident with the police. She had red waist-long hair and hazel eyes, and a strength and resolve to her, despite the growling match.

"Do you have any idea what it did to me to have my wife thrown on the ground in front of me and cuffed? We were dancing in the living room—I was dancing in my underwear—when they came to my door and threw me down."

"Sean," I said. "Please tell us all your grievances and why you want to shut down this longstanding ministry." I knew he needed to be heard.

"The hikers throw trash on my property. They come to my door in the middle of the night, drunk, high, tripping out—and I know what that looks like—not knowing where the hell they are. I've had enough. I'm sick and tired of it. I've been patient and tolerant, but this has gone too far," he said with a loud voice. "I'm going to see to it that this ends today."

I sensed David's growing anger. Bonnie sat on the love seat behind Lena, quietly observing.

"Sean," I said calmly, "I understand you're upset, and I understand why. We weren't aware of these issues until now, and we can take measures to help solve these problems."

He pounded his hand on the table. "I want to speak to that hiker who called the police!"

David said she had hiked out earlier that morning and was not available.

"I want to speak to her," Sean repeated.

David repeated himself, this time with an edge to his voice.

After a few more rounds of verbal stoning, I said to Sean, "It seems to me that we can do a couple of things to ensure peace when our hikers are here. For one, we can post private property signs all along the edge of your property. We can also prohibit hikers from camping near your property line. Would that help?"

I watched as Sean visibly softened. His lips relaxed, as did his posture. "Yes, yes, that would help," he said.

"We can do that," I said. "Can we try to see if this helps?"

It was impossible not to feel Sean's disquiet, his sense of dislocation, and inner turmoil.

The meeting ended shortly after the promise we made to take such measures. I thanked Sean and Lena for coming to us and promised we'd do what we could to ensure their peace and privacy. I watched as they walked away, closer together than when they had arrived, Sean's gait less mechanical. Lena lit a cigarette.

A few weeks later, I was eating lunch with a few other pastors at a favorite local bikers' bar. Sean was there, belting down a couple of beers, although at first, I didn't realize it was him.

"I was wondering when you'd recognize me," Sean called out across the room, drawing everyone's attention halfway through lunch.

"It took me a minute—but I asked myself, who's that good-looking guy at the bar?" I laughed, and so did he.

When I finished eating, I sidled up next to him and asked how he was doing.

"I'm avoiding going home to cut firewood," he said. He sat where he could visually scan the restaurant, his back toward no one.

I attempted to discern if there was tension between us. Maybe the alcohol had anesthetized him somewhat, or the measures we had taken to secure his property had appeased him. He proceeded to tell me about his "messed up" family, how he never wanted kids, that he knew he wasn't father material. He spoke of the war. Then he stood up, motioning for me to follow to a wall of photographs featuring members of the area's armed forces.

"That's me," he said, pointing to one of a soldier wearing a helmet, a scarf over his mouth, sunglasses shielding his eyes, sitting in a Hummer with an M-4 Carbine rifle in hand. "I haven't been in the service for several years, but I can't escape it."

We returned to our seats, where he continued to guzzle his third beer.

I said, "Sean, I've never been to combat, although I did cover some of Operation Desert Storm as a journalist years ago. I've done a few military stories, but I've been thinking a lot about trauma in general, and I have a theory. I'd like to share it with you, and maybe you can tell me if it rings true."

"Go ahead," he said, but I could see his defenses slip into place as if I were trespassing some sacred ground.

"I don't think we were made to endure stuff like war and killing.

We're not built for it, not built for other stuff, too, like abuse or betrayal. It fractures us on the inside, and even time doesn't heal it or heal it well enough. Think we were made for love, that's all."

Sean was silent. He reached again for his beer. "You're right," he said. "I keep trying to put the war behind me. I keep telling myself to look forward, to stop looking back."

"It's like we keep perpetuating the very thing that is destroying us," I said. "I think it's our way of trying to heal ourselves, to desensitize ourselves, like we're trying to take the pain out of it, but we can't; it's always there. Sometimes I don't think our spirit ever finds a way to reattach itself. I think only God can do that if we let Him."

Sean stood up. His face had paled.

We hugged. I felt a pounding at his ribs, and thought that he had been at war long before he was deployed; does any soldier come home the same as when they left for war?

"I'm here for you, Sean, whenever you want to talk. I'll be here next week at the same time if you want to continue the conversation."

He said he'd be back next week.

He wasn't.

I didn't speak with him again for several months, but I saw him at a distance, a shadow among bare winter trees. I'd hear the burst and high-pitched whine of the chainsaw rupturing the solitude, the crack of an ax as he cut and split wood. I prayed for him to find the grace that flows into broken places.

TIN MAN AND EINSTEIN

I think you are wrong to want a heart. It makes most people unhappy. If you only knew it, you are in luck not to have a heart.

L. Frank Baum

April 13, 2016

"No pain, no gain, no Maine," said Einstein, as he collected his newly organized gear and stuffed them into his pack after having slept the night in the center. He had started his trek from Springer Mountain, Georgia, on January 15.

Outside, the sky was anemic even though the rain had eased up, and it was shivering cold. Fellow hiker Tin Man was taking a zero-day. He and Einstein had hiked on and off together over the last three months, but Tin Man said his legs couldn't take the stress of Pennsylvania's sharp rocks, and he needed to rest.

"I was only on the trail for two days when I had to get off for six. I just overdid it. I couldn't even walk up a flight of stairs," Tin Man said.

Einstein was slight of build, had copper-colored hair, a few long chin hairs, but nothing one might call a real beard, freckles, and eyes the color you wished the sky always was. I asked why he was walking the AT.

"I wanted to develop a better relationship with myself."

"How's that going?"

"Well, I still have nine hundred miles to go. I've gained a lot of confidence, especially starting in winter. I had to figure out how to survive. I kept telling myself I can do this. I think the most important thing I've learned is if I can do this, I don't need to listen to people who say you can't do this or that in my life."

Both Einstein and Tin Man had graduated from their respective colleges in December. Hiking the AT was a gift they gave themselves before moving on to write the next chapter of their lives. For Einstein, graduating with a degree in math and physics (how he earned his trail name) meant starting a five-year PhD program in climate dynamics and atmospherics in the fall.

Tin Man, who graduated with a mechanical engineering degree, would begin working at a Fortune 500 company in September. They shared how neither set of parents was happy about their sons' decision to abandon all for the trail for five to six months, but both parents didn't stop them either.

"They were worried about me, they had heard all the horror stories, but I reminded them that the trail is safer than any city," Tin Man said.

"Hiking the AT has taught me that you don't need a lot to live," Einstein continued, eager to talk as he fetched the rest of his stuff. "In 'real life'"—he made quotation marks in the air—"you think you need this and that. When you're backpacking, you're forced to get rid of what you don't need. The key is to remember that you don't need a lot and not get caught up thinking I need this, and I need that. I don't want to carry that weight in my head. If you can't carry it on your shoulders, you don't have to have it."

"I hope you will write that on your bones as you both begin careers and enter the acquiring stage of life," I said, thinking how it is that I was in the stage of life of giving away—myself, my stuff, my hard-earned lessons, of downsizing and simplifying.

"I started in January so that I could walk alone and not in a bubble," Einstein said.

Tin Man agreed as he sat on the couch and started to massage his sore legs. He was a spindly young man with dark chocolate eyes and hair, fair skin, and an impressively thick and curly beard long enough to hide his entire neck.

"I've had a lot of time to think on the trail. Before, I was afraid to be alone and to think on my own. I used to say I was lonely but not anymore," Tin Man said.

"What has the trail taught you?" I asked him just before Einstein stepped out of the center to make a phone call.

"I've learned that I don't want to put so much emphasis on work, on climbing the corporate ladder. For the next three years, the company will send me to three different locations to learn three different aspects of the business, training me in management. I'm going to ask them if I can take time off in between rotations. I doubt it's been done before, but I am going to try. I want to keep hiking; there are several trails out there, the Pacific Crest Trail, John Muir Trail, the Continental Divide," Tin Man continued.

"This seems to be consistent with your generation, wanting the balance of work and play. My parents, who grew up during the Depression, placed a great deal of emphasis on hard work and having large families. My generation focused on affluence, at least until the Great Recession happened. It'll be interesting to see how the workforce shifts in the years to come. By the way, how did you get the name Tin Man?" I asked.

"The name Tin Man originated from the industrial revolution when people left their farms for manufacturing—it was a newspaper joke, a name for the man who became part of the great machine, who had lost his heart. I don't want to become the Tin Man, to lose heart. I don't want corporate life to remove what's most important to me, working for the machine all day." Tin Man paused, then asked, "What made you want to be a pastor?"

"Not many hikers ask me that question. I'm curious why you ask; had you ever thought about going into the ministry?"

"No, except my father wanted me to be a Serbian priest. You asked me, so I thought I would ask you."

His question struck me as an unexpected act of generosity. Most hikers don't ask unless they are considering such a vocation. I have often thought that to ask me why I became a minister is to open the door to a conversation that most are uncomfortable having. After all, we're taught to stay away from discussing politics and religion. Besides, if a person listens, it might unsettle them since it was my restlessness, what

I call my holy discontentment, that forced me to reconsider my life, its meaning, where my fulfillment came from, and what was the next chapter for me to write as I entered mid-life. Religion is too personal, some say. I say this is especially true of Christianity that invites others to engage with a too-personal God.

I answered, "I've had two passions in my life—theology and writing. I was a journalist for twenty years and was able to travel extensively. I wrote novels that didn't see the light of day, went through a divorce, remarried, and had another child at forty, making three in my brood. All this to say that I came to a place in my mid-forties where I knew I had to shift. The thing is, I grew up in a church where women weren't allowed to be ordained. I started to attend a Presbyterian church, and I remember hearing a guest woman minister preach one morning. I kept thinking all through her sermon that I should stick my fingers in my ears so that I don't listen. Makes me laugh now."

Tin Man's eyes fixated on mine; he seemed intent on listening, so I continued.

"You know, there was a deep knowing inside me. I can't explain it, never have been able to explain it, but there was an undeniable force pushing me to pursue the ministry. So I went back to school and earned my Masters of Divinity degree and was ordained nine years ago. Of course, there's a lot more to it, but that's how I came to make a major life change." I paused. "Can you tell me about your father wanting you to be a priest?"

"My father wanted me to be a Serbian Orthodox priest. I grew up going to a Serbian church in Chicago where mass is still said in ancient Serbian. My father's from Serbia, and we spoke the language at home. My parents divorced when I was young, and my dad moved back to Serbia when I was in high school. I've spent a lot of time there and will go back before I start my job in the fall. He has a farm. Farming is quite lucrative there, unlike here."

"So, no desire in you to become a priest?"

"None," he said.

I chuckled. "I have to say, Tin Man, I appreciate your openness and our conversation."

"I think it comes from being on the trail, from listening to myself when no one else is around. At the end of a long day on the trail, when hikers collapse for the night and sit around a campfire, the conversations are usually pretty real. We're too tired to keep our walls up; they just come tumbling down. We're too tired to pretend; being tired takes everything away."

"What do you mean, 'takes everything away?'"

"Everything that stands in the way of telling another who you truly are," he said.

"It's safe too; chances are you won't see most of them again," I added.

Einstein came back into the center just then, the phone still pinned to his ear. With one hand, he placed the last items into his pack, then said goodbye, and slipped the phone into his pant pocket. He tightened the cord of his pack, then lifted it to his back.

"See you down the trail, Tin Man." He turned to me and said, "Thanks for all you do for hikers. This is a great place to stay." He headed out the door; a rush of cool, rain-scented air pushed inside behind him.

I left Tin Man shortly after Einstein left. The two would most likely meet up again, not far down the trail. I imagined them walking alone, listening to the voice within them, clear and true, and all their own. When they completed their hike, I wondered if they would still hear it, if they would obey it, if hiking day after day for months finally broke the sound barrier within them once and for all.

TRAIL LEGS

Definition: The point where hikers' bodies adjust to the daily grind of thru-hiking and their legs gain the strength and stamina for high mileage days.[3]

H E HAD A BAMBOO HEART—STRAIGHT and strong, resilient, hollow in the middle.

I had just returned from a three-week journey to Kenya. I interviewed and photographed orphans and vulnerable children helped by Alice Visionary Foundation Project, a ministry headquartered in Kisumu. Back home now, I was grateful to breathe and bask in the autumn air against a scrim of fallen leaves, even though Africa was still aflame in my bones.

I was surprised to find anyone in the dimly-lit Hikers Center in mid-November, being late in the hiking season. Quadzilla was there alone, sitting on the couch, sorting through a resupply box filled with food and other essentials on the coffee table in front of him. A 35mm Canon camera was balanced at his side—an unusual sight, as hikers rarely carried so bulky and heavy a camera. I imagined he was someone who wanted to pay attention to the details, who didn't want to forget what he saw or what he did, who wanted to create a visible map of his trek, proof of his accomplishment.

Southbound from Mt. Katahdin, he told me he would finish his hike in West Virginia. He had flip-flopped the first part of the trail months earlier, starting at Springer Mountain, Georgia, hiking to Harper's Fer-

---

3   https://www.northeasthikes.com/hiking-dictionary/

ry, West Virginia. Then he had traveled to Maine to walk southbound back to Harper's Ferry.

A red bandana, looped around the young man's head, grazed his eyeglasses' upper rim and forced his jet black hair upward into a messy crown. He had earned the trail name Quadzilla, he said, for the size of his quads after hiking for a few weeks. At twenty-nine years old, he had his own online business he conducted while on the trail, helping gamers addicted to playing video games by providing nutrition and fitness programs to break the same addiction he had once suffered.

"I'd been playing video games from the time I was fifteen until I was twenty-two years old. I had stopped going to all my classes in college, spending most of my day playing. I realized that I was escaping and avoiding my life, and I decided to stop playing so much, get outdoors, work out, and not let it control me anymore."

"Did you figure out why you were avoiding your life?" I asked.

He became perfectly still then as if what he was about to say required every bit of his strength and concentration. "My parents were university professors in China; they were involved in political protests, and my father was sentenced to prison. At the time, two American professors were lecturing at the university. He asked them to bring me to the United States to find me a family. The Americans knew of a woman in their hometown in Kansas who had wanted to adopt a child, so they brought me to the United States, and a single white woman adopted me."

I sat silently on the edge of the coffee table as he spoke, waiting for him to say more. Still, there was an awkward pause, so I said, "I can't imagine how difficult that must have been for your parents—they must have been scared to death as to what might happen to you if you had stayed in China. I can't imagine how traumatic that must have been for you if you were old enough to remember."

"I was eight; I remember everything." He turned his face away from me to stare out the window, drawn to the light that shone through.

"I am so, so sorry that you had to go through that. I seriously can't even imagine the impact this has had on you."

"I don't remember feeling anything. I tell people that I became independent at the age of eight." There was no hint of his mother tongue as if his first language slept somewhere else in his body.

"Quadzilla," I said, "I think I get why you said you became independent at eight, taken away from everything you knew, from your parents, your country, your home. Did you keep your Chinese name?"

"My adoptive mother took my name away from me and renamed me Jack Smith. The name I knew myself as was Li Chao Kim." He seemed to swallow his name, tucking it back into his throat, where no one else could claim it.

"I can't help but ask, did you ever find out what happened to your parents?"

"My father was released from prison after two years, and he and my mother came to America and settled in my town, but my adoptive mother would not give me back to them. I didn't see them much. When I was thirteen, my father died. I don't know what of, but he took all kinds of Chinese medicine. I saw him only three times before he died, even though they had lived near me for almost three years."

Did he die of a crushed spirit, exiled from his son's life? I didn't ask.

He continued, his voice contained, without inflections. "My mother remarried after my father died, and she had a son with her second husband, but I don't see her much. I am not close to her. I'm not that close to my adoptive mother, either."

"It's like you belonged to everybody and nobody, you know what I mean?"

He half-nodded as if he agreed. "I joined the Army in search of a masculine influence and for male bonding. I would listen to men cry in their bunks at night because they were homesick and missed their families. I never cried; I was never homesick."

"Maybe because you feel like home was stolen from you twenty years ago. Maybe that's what trauma does, leaves us with terrible, deep homesickness for the self. I've suffered it myself in life, learned that forgiveness helped; I had to forgive others as well as myself."

"I don't know. Maybe I haven't forgiven my parents or my adoptive mother." He shifted his weight, reached for his camera, carefully wrapped it, and then stuffed it into his pack.

"I often ask hikers when they come here what they've learned by being on the trail. Some say how little they need to survive; others say self-reliance. What about you?"

"Mostly, that we are all more limitless than we think. We place limits on ourselves, on what we think we can do, or how we should live. I never thought I could hike the trail or complete it, but I realized that I could do so much more than I thought. When I go back home, I want to speak at schools and talk to young people about challenging themselves to go further than they think they can, to push themselves harder and not let them, or anyone else, tell them what they are or aren't capable of doing, or achieving."

"To not limit or avoid their own life, it sounds like you are saying," I said. "You're the first hiker to put it in those words, in that way, I think. I wish someone had shared that with me when I was younger. I mean, we aren't limitless, but we do impose so many limits on ourselves. So, what do you see yourself doing over the next part of your life? I mean, is this how you picture your ideal life?"

"I would like to travel, maybe buy a van, take my camera and photograph, take videos, write and do speaking engagements."

"Do you see yourself traveling solo?"

"I have a girlfriend, but yes, I see myself doing it alone."

He had a bamboo heart—straight and strong, resilient, hollow in the middle, where all possibility lies, where forgiveness waits, where the echo of grown men's cries might be heard, where homesickness waits for God, the seemingly prodigal Father.

TREES

Above all, do not lose your desire to walk.
Every day I walk myself into a state of well-being,
and walk away from every illness.
I have walked myself into my best thoughts,
and I know of no thought so burdensome
that one cannot walk away from it.

Søren Kierkegaard

Entry from the center's Hiker Journal, dated April 25, 2016:

"Nearly four years ago, I decided to stop my thru-hike (SOBO) here at the Church of the Mountain. I had had enough. But I am back as I think I always knew I would be, to continue south. A little hesitant to leave 'the world' behind but I feel that there is peace not far into the trees. (BTW that last line is not intended to sound like a suicide note)."
Sticks

I hadn't met Sticks. Likely, he had come and gone when I wasn't at church, but I imagined him tall and thin and breakable. Maybe he had given himself the name; from the sound of his writings, he sounded like someone a bit disconnected from himself, not an uncommon feeling for many.

"Peace not far into the trees"—he'd find it, if he listened, I was confident, as the magnolia and dogwood and lilac were resurrecting from the dead, sweetening the air. If he listened, would he hear the cambium humming its own song; oaks their croon, maples their anthem, birches their ballads?

Half a dozen hikers were flocking into the center daily now. The last two weeks of brilliant sun and bluest sky brought with it an early spring exuberance. With the increasing numbers expected over the summer, the church decided to begin the Hikers Feed two weeks earlier, in mid-May. This year we were celebrating forty years of the Hikers Ministry, and we were planning various ways to acknowledge this unique, often taxing, ministry of hospitality. We preached not with words but with fresh tomatoes, pasta salad, fresh green beans, southern fried chicken, and succulent watermelons, knowing that feeding the body feeds the soul.

I scrolled through the journal and read another entry, written in three separate lines, dated April 26, the following day:

"'True freedom is to know your nature and live in accordance with it.'" Quote attributed to John C. Wright, an American writer.

"Surely then the nature of man is an ultimately spiritual being. Why would we dream of better and greater than the rare material, if there was nothing else? That seems counter-intuitive."

"'It takes great faith to believe that a phenomenon of the scale and complexity of the observable universe was a mere accident.'"

* * *

Mid-afternoon, hurrying out of my office to attend a meeting, I noticed a tent pitched outside Fellowship House. No one was in sight, but there was gear alongside it. Before I turned around, a man in a star-spangled kerchief, earrings, and well-worn clothes, with a pit bull by his side, startled me.

He explained that he had started a month earlier in Harper's Ferry, West Virginia. He called himself Flip for flip-flopping the trail. Once he reached the trail's end at Mt. Katahdin, Maine, he would rent a car, travel to Springer Mountain, Georgia, and walk the trail up to Harper's Ferry, completing his journey.

"It wasn't so long ago that I was in a wheelchair. I couldn't walk," he said. "I have multiple sclerosis. Still have a lot of neuropathy in my face, legs, and hands, making hiking difficult, but I'm doing it. I'm walking for the MS Foundation that helps those who live with the disease."

He appeared much older than forty-nine, the age he claimed, probably due to his white beard and the long, deep quotation lines around his eyes. Maybe the disease had aged him. I remembered someone explaining what it felt like to have MS, saying it felt like you were walking on balloons.

"I wrote a book about a woman with MS. I can't wait to tell her what you're doing; you're an inspiration. How are you managing on the trail?"

"I'm doing really well despite my neuropathy. I'm in the God-made out there, not the man-made. I don't take conventional medicine for MS. My medicine is being in the woods, kicking leaves, inhaling the air and sun."

"Hikers tell me all the time about how being on the trail has helped cured them of all kinds of things, of loneliness and trauma, and improved their overall health, both physically and spiritually. I even read an article recently about how scientists see changes in the brain when we're out and about in nature."

We talked for a few more minutes, but I had to leave to make my meeting on time. He asked me for a hug. I had a pastor friend who told me that as a male, he could not initiate a hug, but a female pastor can do so easily, as it's interpreted differently. Since there was no one else around, I hesitated, but then I laced my arms around him for a brief hug, feeling a slight tremor radiate up through him. I felt the notches of his spine beneath my hands; when he released his hold, it was as if bits of him came off on me.

"*Peace not far into the trees*," Sticks wrote in the journal.

Flip was like a tree, bent and broken, splintered almost, yet whole. I heard the underground groans in him and felt him shudder as if a storm couldn't find a way out of him.

POSTLUDE TO TREES

As I drove away, I recalled my mother, now in her nineties, reminiscing about when she was a young girl. She'd go into the apple orchard alongside her house, cradling her baby doll, lugging a blanket that she'd spread over the ground, and place her tea set upon. She would sit among the trees. Each tree had a name—Emily, Elizabeth, Mary—and she would greet them in the morning and talk to them about little girl things not overheard inside the family house. In the shade, sometimes sprawled out on the bare earth, she'd watch as the wind fluttered through the branches and leaves. Blossoms would fall upon her like pink rain in spring, sunlight like seeds, planting themselves under her skin. The green ripening globes, growing so large and red out of the king blossom right in front of her, were small secret worlds. She'd wonder about the branches, split, pressed, and wrapped into each other, what her father called a graft.

When the apples blushed in September, she'd no longer come out in the early morning, afraid of the strange hobos who would come and pick apples off the ground. Then the forlorn men would walk toward the house and knock on the back kitchen door, begging for food, as it was during the Depression then. Her mother would give them some food but shut the door fast behind her.

Maybe that is why the trees call from forests and orchards and groves. They invite in. They have no doors to shut anyone out.

TRESPASS

I don't trust a man who hasn't suffered; I don't let a man get close to me who hasn't faced his wound. Think of the posers you know—are they the kind of man you would call at 2:00 A.M., when life is collapsing around you? Not me. I don't want clichés; I want deep, soulful truth, and that only comes when a man has walked the road I've been talking about.

John Eldredge

I T WAS AN OVERHEATED, STICKY Saturday evening. The humidity exaggerated the fungi-odor of wet boots, sweat-stained shirts, shorts, kilts, and gear. I tried not to breathe through my nose. I promised myself if I stayed for a while inside the center, I wouldn't be so overwhelmed by the stink. A dozen packs, scattered over the floor and in the bunk room, smudged and streaked by rain and dirt, had crossed hiking poles leaning against them like skulls and crossbones. Food separated into small plastic bags was scattered here and there from opened resupply boxes. The hikers' box, where stuff is left for the taking, overflowed with all kinds of items, including a tent, sleeping bag, sunglasses, maps, and a transistor radio.

Only one hiker was inside, sitting on the couch cross-legged, reading a book, with a fan just a foot away, tilted and blowing on him. He appeared to be in his mid-forties. His hair was dark and thick but short and trimmed. By the looks of his beard, I guessed he had been on the trail for months. Yet, he seemed too round to have been hiking for that long unless he had started out a lot larger. He wore a fluorescent tee shirt and a kilt; his exposed legs were covered with bug bites, a few scrapes, and gashes.

"I've been section-hiking with a few of my friends," he said. "I've done everything south of here years before. We started in Unionville, but I can't go any further—it kicked my butt. It's too much for me; I can't take it. We were hiking fifteen miles a day. My buddies are still out there; we're going to rendezvous soon and head home. I'm hanging around until they meet me here if that's ok?"

"Yes, of course," I said. "Are you injured?"

"No, only my pride. Thought I could do it. Just suffering some disappointment in myself."

Home was Indiana. His olive skin had ripened in the week he had been outdoors. Eyes, a deep brown, his gaze was steady and warm. His beard and mustache hid his lips but provided a contrasting scrim to his straight, white teeth.

As we talked, I learned he had been a lawyer who believed in a God of justice—that alone was intriguing enough. He'd left his law practice nine years earlier to become a teacher at a classical Christian School.

"It's a school that teaches the classics and organizes education around the child's developmental stages. For example, I teach Latin to elementary students. We memorize, sing, and do rhymes to learn Latin. By the time students reach high school, they're in a different stage—they want to argue—so we teach them how to argue rhetorically, engage in an exchange with people non-emotively or personally. Seniors have to write a fifteen-page persuasive paper and defend it in front of a board," he explained.

"Latin, huh?" I grunted. "I can't help but ask what made you choose to leave law. That doesn't often happen, you know, the golden handcuffs kind of thing."

"I had read John Eldredge's book, *Wild at Heart*. It was the most influential book in my life, next to the Bible. Eldredge writes about how the male heart is wired and how we're pulled toward that thing that makes us feel most alive. It wasn't law; it was teaching that made me feel most alive. It was what I loved most about my work as a lawyer when I had to educate others."

"That's quite a transition."

"I knew I couldn't or wouldn't do it without my wife's support, and she said, 'if your passion is to teach, then teach.' I prayed about it, believing that this was the path I was to pursue. God said, 'Well, yes, but not yet.' We had two young daughters, and we needed to figure out a way to afford the career change."

"I imagine it took a lot of courage," I said.

He nodded and continued in his tenor voice: "It did and more than I had at the time. Before I could leave my practice, I had to pay off a debt of almost a hundred thousand dollars that my partner messed me over with."

As he continued, what became evident in his story is how the path from being a lawyer to an educator, like all the journeys it seems God urges us to embark upon, starts with an exodus. There is a wilderness to trod, and the destination one finally reaches is never final. God moves, and so must we.

"What I had to learn through this journey from one career to another was forgiveness. What happened with my partner taught me how to release my forgiveness, to move forward, beyond it, to deal with it. I didn't have to be the hand of justice. That was God's place, not mine. I didn't know it at the time, but the lessons I learned through all of that, the betrayal and dishonesty, and learning to forgive my ex-partner, prepared me for what happened this last year." He cast his gaze down. "Something happened at school, and I had to choose to forgive." He looked up but away from me. "It happened with my daughter, which is always harder than if it just happened to me. But because of what I'd learned years earlier, I could release the person who had harmed her. 'Surely we are born for trouble as readily as sparks fly up from a fire,'" he said, quoting from the Book of Job. "We confronted the person, told her she had done wrong, that we chose to forgive—I don't know if she chose to hear that, but we had to say it."

"Makes you wonder, doesn't it, about why our journeys always seem to take so long?" I said.

"Something beautiful came out of what had happened to my daughter," he confided. "My wife and I developed a deeper relationship with her. She's more forthcoming; she's listening to us rather than to social media."

"Don't you wonder if by this happening to her, this stumbling block may have kept her from falling off some cliff later—just like what happened to you?"

He was silent for a moment as if we were in a court of law, and I had drawn a conclusion he hadn't seen coming. "You may be right, as hard as it's to accept. Life's messy, and being a Christian makes it more difficult. There are no shortcuts."

Ruminating on the thought of no shortcuts, I said, "Are you struggling with forgiving yourself for feeling like the trail beat you this time around?"

"I am," he said. "I called my wife, told her I had to get off the trail, and I'm struggling with feeling so disappointed in myself. She reminded me of a quote by Theodore Roosevelt."

He recited it, word for word: "'It isn't the critic who counts; not the man who points out how the strong man stumbles, or where the doer of deeds could have done them better. The credit belongs to the man who is actually in the arena, whose face is marred by dust and sweat and blood; who strives valiantly; who errs, who comes short again and again, because there is no effort without error and shortcoming; but who does actually strive to do the deeds; who knows great enthusiasms, the great devotions; who spends himself in a worthy cause; who at the best knows in the end the triumph of high achievement, and who at the worst, if he fails, at least fails while daring greatly, so that his place shall never be with those cold and timid souls who neither know victory nor defeat.'"

Both of us were quiet for a moment. I questioned if such revelations were all a part of the trail—how maybe it has to defeat you before you can conquer it; something within has to take over, something beyond courage, even beyond grit; something like faith, something like surrender. After all, trail and trial are practically the same word.

I glanced at the open book sprawled across his lap, imagining the words on the page were tiny insects that flew up off the page and around his head, wings buzzing with reminders of what he perceived as his defeat, like annoying mosquito-thoughts impossible to swat dead.

"I suppose all our journeys include forgiving ourselves," I said, even though I wanted to ask if he worried that his heart was not wild enough in his aging, over-tamed body.

"Eldredge would say I'm becoming more trustworthy through suffering."

"You've left me with stuff to think about, thank you," I said.

It was getting late. Hikers returned from town and began to hunker down, making intimate conversation difficult, so I said goodnight after inviting him to join us for worship the next morning. He said he would come. I named him Latin before leaving the center.

The following morning he came to church and sat in the back of the sanctuary along with a few other hikers. I spoke of how our journeys' circuitous ways prepare us for what will come in the future. And I wondered if forgiving himself for not finishing the hike was preparing him for something later that would come.

TRUE NORTH

*He took the blind man by the hand and led him outside
the village. When he had spit on the man's eyes and put
his hands on him, Jesus asked, "Do you see anything?"
He looked up and said, "I see people; they look like
trees walking around.*

Mark 8:23-24
New International Version

ACCORDING TO A HIKER NAMED Disciple of Jesus, God named
him while he hiked the trail the summer of 2015; it wasn't a
name he or anyone else gave him. He didn't receive it while hiking
northbound or reached the summit of Mt. Katahdin, but only when he
did a U-turn on that summit and headed southbound.

"I hadn't learned to listen. I kept questioning, 'God, what do you
want me to do next?'"

His name elicited instant judgment, I thought, in a world that
judges anyone so bold to carry such a label.

Disciple of Jesus returned to the church in mid-October after having stayed here in the first week of June when he arrived just in time
for the first Hiker Feed of the season.

"Truly, it was the best meal I've had the entire time I have been
walking for the last eight months," he told us.

It was a mild fall day when he returned, after two freezing nights on
the trail. The trees were still clutching their copper and tangerine colors. He had been sitting with earphones in his ears, his eyes fastened to
his tiny cell phone screen. Such was not an uncommon sight—hikers

listening to music, muffling the noise of the rest of the world, missing out on the crackle of brittle leaves, and the creak of bending branches, or voices all around.

A Boston Red Sox baseball cap hid his hair and half his forehead; he was wearing black Under Armour leggings, a black long sleeve shirt beneath a pair of shorts, and a short sleeve top. Dark blue eyeglass frames magnified the indigo color of his eyes. He had a reddish beard a few inches long with spikes of gray and white, not unruly or overpowering as most hikers had by the time they reached here that hid the contours of their faces.

There was something about the forty-three-year-old hiker that I couldn't articulate, only that he seemed adrift as if he'd lost his inner compass. Maybe it was just my reaction to his turning around after walking twenty-two hundred miles and walking back as if he had nowhere else to go. True, hikers are homeless on the trail, but not all were pilgrims as he appeared to be, or as one hiker had said to me, "homeless with a purpose."

"Where's your family live?" I inquired.

"My parents live in southern Maine."

I guessed from his response but did not verify that there probably wasn't any wife or children or job waiting for him. I asked him what was different now that he was going southbound.

"I'm not worried about myself anymore. When I was northbound, I focused on Mt. Katahdin, on the finish line, and what I experienced. When I climbed the summit, it was an emotional experience for me. Going southbound, I am just listening."

"What are you hearing?"

"I can't explain it. I'm walking, but I'm still inside. Sometimes I find myself with tears running down my face. All my focus is on God now, not on finishing the trail, not on Mt. Katahdin, not even on one foot in front of the other. I feel God's hand upon me all the time. There are no distractions on the trail—it's me, God, the wilderness."

"I think maybe we all have to find God in the wilderness first, or we never really find him at all," I said.

"What do you mean?"

"Just that if we find God in the wilderness, in the waterless places, when we are all alone, we never lose him."

"I found Christ when I was thirty. My life was pretty much in the gutter then. It started when my coworker gave me a Bible. He didn't tell me much, just handed it to me. I read it, and it was like my eyes popped wide open. I saw the way life was supposed to be lived; I just tried to follow Jesus' teaching, but I fell away."

"What happened?"

In the short time it took for him to gather his thoughts, I remembered my own "falling away" when I no longer felt I was acceptable to God. The first time was when as a virgin I was date-raped at age fifteen. The second was when I went through a divorce—I had failed the most fundamental things in life, I thought then. What mercy and grace were left for me? I had spent plenty of time in the wilderness and in desert places during these times, and plenty of other times, but even in those parched and lonely places, I searched to hear God call my name once again. I discovered there could be a spring of living water flowing into me only if I let contaminated water flow out of me.

"I moved to Clearwater, Florida; that was the beginning of it," he continued. "I started dealing drugs with my cousin, started doing ecstasy, and a bunch of other stuff." He shook his head as if in disbelief, then said, "I hit rock bottom fast—within a few months. When I was there in Clearwater, there was an abandoned insurance building. One day an iridescent image of Mother Mary holding Baby Jesus appeared on the mirrored glass three stories high. I passed by it every day. A church started there, and then a few years later, someone fired gunshots at it one night, and it shattered. I remember people crying and how the shattered glass glistened like water, catching the light, reflecting so many colors—purple, green, yellow." Disciple of Jesus seemed to float away for a moment.

"I don't remember hearing about that."

"That image had been a constant reminder that I wasn't alone and that I wasn't doing the right thing."

"Did you go into rehab or go to a recovery program?" I asked.

"No, Jesus just took my desire for drugs away. Never had a desire to do drugs again."

"Wow," I said. "Do you share your story with other hikers?"

"Most of them want nothing to do with organized religion. They don't want to hear about Jesus; they only want to develop their spirituality, their religion. It's like they treat organized religion as if it's organized crime."

I chuckled. "Unfortunately, there have been too many crimes committed in the name of religion. I taught Comparative Religions at college, and this idea of being spiritual and not religious was expressed by most of the students. So I asked them to write about what 'disorganized religion' might look like. I think that most people want to name themselves; they don't want to carry around someone else's name, like Christ's name."

"They mock me, but it's okay. I pray for them, and it feels pretty good. Jesus says to love your enemies and pray for those who persecute you, right?"

We were interrupted, and I had to leave for a meeting. In parting, he said, "I don't know what's next for me, but all I care about is walking with Him. I only want to focus on the here and now."

The AT had been a Damascus Road for Disciple of Jesus as it had for other hikers. Only he was blinded to anything else but the Presence. Having gone south, he found his True North.

UNREQUITED LOVE

The eternal makes you urgent.

John O'Donohue

TEDDY BEAR WAS GIVEN HIS trail name by fellow hiker Grizzly in the summer of 2018. He had a sunless complexion, a reddish beard, and a head of unkempt blond hair. There was a kind of absence and sadness in his eyes. When he directed his gaze at me, it took time for him to focus on my face.

"Would you send me out with a good spiritual thought this morning? I'm waiting for my phone to download an audiobook," he said as I stepped out of my pickup truck in front of Fellowship House.

"You came to church yesterday morning. You're from Oregon, right?"

"Yes," he said, then paused as if he was fishing for words he couldn't reel in.

"Are you a churchgoer?" I asked.

"No, I'm Jewish," he said, "but there wasn't any synagogue around." He looked away. "I cried during the service."

"During my sermon, I hope!"

"No."

I winced.

"I cried when the people were praying out loud for those by name," he said. "I prayed for a friend of mine." He shifted his gaze and seemed to slip away.

"Oh," I said. "So you want a good spiritual thought? I was just reflecting on a recent medical mission trip to Cuba."

I felt the words rise in me, wanting to stifle the silence that too often leaves me feeling adrift. They came in sentences, fast and passionate, and I wanted to apologize for my rush even before I spoke.

"I've been thinking a lot about a pastor I met there, Raimundo Garcia Franco. He had been a guerrilla fighter for Castro, then part of Castro's Radicalization Movement, when he had to confiscate land and businesses from his countrymen.

"In time, he became disillusioned by what he saw and experienced. Eventually, he became a minister. But when Castro aligned with the USSR, the church had to go underground. Raimundo was too outspoken. So he, along with many other ministers, Catholic high school students, criminals, and homosexuals, were sent to a labor camp for two years, working on the same sugar plantations that he had burned when he was fighting for Castro."

I stopped for a moment to make sure I hadn't buried him beneath my verbiage. He brought his unblinking gaze back toward me, so I continued.

"After his release, he wanted to start a dialogue with the government to stop the persecution of the church, but the denomination he was serving refused to support him, so he quit. Long story short, out of his suffering and experience in the labor camp, he had a vision for what God wanted him to do with his life. He established a center for dialogue and reflection and social justice that draws people from all over the world."

He stared into me. I wondered if it was the labor camp, the religious and the irreligious imprisoned together, that stirred him.

I said, "The thought I was mulling around is how sometimes it is out of our suffering that the greatest vision for our lives comes if we don't run from it."

"Christianity glorifies suffering," he said slowly, not moving his eyes from mine.

"It has in some ways," I agreed.

"I've suffered unrequited love my whole life. It's been a pattern for me. I was in love with a woman, but she ended up sleeping with my best friend. I was praying out loud for him yesterday, during the service."

"Have you forgiven him?" I pictured him falling in love with young women from both a physical and psychic distance. Did these women know he was in love with them? How could they respond if he never told them? Can anyone love someone truly that they don't know?

"I don't think I was there for him when his parents were going through a divorce. I don't think I took his pain seriously. Maybe that's why he did it."

His body was motionless. It seemed as if he was listening to someone inside of him.

"I've been depressed most of my life. Suicidal, really."

I waited for him to say more, but he didn't. I asked, "How are you managing depression on the trail? Hikers tell me being on the trail is the best thing they've ever done for their mental health."

"When darkness comes, so does depression. I wake up before it's light, start to walk among the trees, the sun comes up, and depression leaves me."

Just saying the word *depression* felt too heavy even for my tongue to lift.

"I was evaluated for bipolar, depression, all kinds of things, but I refuse medication. I think my generation will be the one that refuses to walk around all drugged up."

"I know something about bipolar disorder as someone I love very much has suffered it all her life. I understand that no one wants to walk around all drugged up, but taking something to balance out the body isn't the same thing as being drugged up, is it?"

"I want to be awake," he said.

"For some, it's the only way to be awake. Some people are drugged up to avoid suffering. Maybe that gets back to Franco, who used his suffering to keep others from having to suffer what he did."

It was as if Teddy Bear went underground.

As I waited for him to emerge, I thought about his confession of unrequited love—the way it seemed to have bruised his heart and made his words come out all black and blue.

He said, "I want to get married," even though he was only twenty years old. He wanted to be loved, to be seen, to be known. I wondered about the girls he had fallen for and if one day they would look back and see him as a gentleman, a teddy bear, and wish they had given him a chance.

"Would you pray for me?" he asked.

I gathered his soft, slender-fingered hands in mine and prayed for him to feel the deep intimate love of God, to experience it in the dark, in the shiver of trees, in the light that breaks dawn into a thousand splinters of sun.

Before I stood up to leave, he showed me the book he was downloading on his phone: the King James Version of the Book of Psalms—a book of lament and anguish, joy and loss, torment and violence, and somehow finding the glory of God in it all. He hugged me goodbye, pressing his spiced hiker scent onto me that I carried for hours afterward.

I thought about unrequited love as he headed down the driveway—the long shadow it casts over a life. I thought about how the joy of requited love sometimes evaporates in the heat of life, shriveling the same heart that was once so enlarged by it. And of God's unrequited love.

I watched as Teddy Bear faded away, as he listened to the poetic prayers of the Psalms. With his every stride, I prayed he'd enter deeper into Eden, hidden in us all.

WARRIORS

Everybody needs beauty as well as bread, places to play in and pray in, where Nature may heal and cheer and give strength to body and souls alike.

John Muir

A FRIEND, ERIC, HAD RETURNED HOME after serving in the Army Special Forces for a decade, and like so many before him, he couldn't find his way back to civilian life, to being the husband and father he wanted to be or expected to be. A part of him was always on the battlefield, leading his unit into unknown territory, where uniforms couldn't identify the enemy. The enemy came disguised as civilian men, women, and children. Discharged honorably from the military six years earlier, he was still struggling with the trauma of war.

"Your soul is like a ball, and every time you do something bad, even if it's for a greater good, a part of it chips away. I was good at being bad. When I came home, my soul was full of holes," he said. "I tried religion, work, therapy, everything. Some of the guys use drugs and alcohol to feel whole again, but nothing so far has worked for me."

"No soul is bulletproof," I said. "No conscience is immune to survivor's guilt."

He repeatedly said: "I was really good at being bad. I have a set of skills for getting the job done."

I dared not ask what those skills were; my imagination filled in the blanks. If I had not known he was ex-military, ex-special ops, I could have guessed it by how he appeared hyper-vigilant.

Red was one of many wounded warriors hiking the trail. He was in his mid-thirties. He was walking as a way to heal from his post-traumatic stress disorder, arriving at the center on a feverish-hot day, having trekked six miles south from the Kirkridge shelter. He earned the trail name, Red, for the halo of strawberry blond hair stubble that enveloped his shaved head. He had a splatter of faded freckles across his cheeks and a metal plate under his scalp—flat and smooth and rectangular that indented his forehead.

Sitting at the picnic table in the shade of the overhang outside the center, he explained, "When I was at Kirkridge, I left my gear and went to get water, about a hundred feet away. When I came back, my wallet was stolen, all my money and identification."

For the next several days, Red bunked here as he reached out to family and friends to get new identification papers, credit cards, and some cash to continue his journey. During that time, he spoke of his brain injury, the shrapnel in his legs, and why he had a permanent limp from an IED. He didn't offer me details about the day the IED exploded, in part, he said, because he had no memory of it.

I couldn't help but imagine scenes of mayhem: blood, lifeless bodies, twisted metal, calls home, reports, white sheets, ascetic smells, his head wrapped in gauze, and recurring nightmares when he spoke. I saw it all in his navy-blue eyes; he barely blinked as he talked, staring into my eyes so intently, I had to avert my gaze.

I have witnessed and partaken of others' trauma as a minister, having held young mothers who were burying their babies, comforted women whose husbands died unexpectedly, and stood by sons as they said goodbye to their fathers. There were strangers in the hospital whom I sang songs to on their deathbeds (praying my voice didn't make them pass more quickly).

Once, a man riding his motorcycle on a warm spring day was hit by a van driven by a teenage boy; I was only two cars behind on the road when it happened. The man lay in the middle of the pavement in a fetal position, unable to move but conscious, saying he couldn't feel his legs. I waited with him for the police and helicopter to fly him to a trauma center, told him I was a minister, and I prayed for him. "My wife is going to kill me," he said over and over again.

The boy behind the wheel of the van was frantically apologizing for hitting the man, saying repeatedly, "I didn't see you. I didn't see you!" He had rolled through a stop sign; the motorcycle was in his blind spot. The injured man, the spiritually-wounded boy—both could have been my husband, my brother, my son.

Another warrior, trail name Just Rick—a name he gave himself—was section-hiking during his two-week vacation. He looked to be in his fifties, had a polite Southern drawl and manners. Stationed in Alabama, he was serving in the Army as a helicopter mechanic. I met him at the post office, next door to the church, where hikers pick up their resupply packages. He had an awful burn scar on his right arm. I asked him about it, wondering if it was from combat.

"When I was six years old, my home caught fire from a television. I passed out and was burned all over my back, the top of my ears and arm. My father was in Vietnam and came home to be with the family and me, probably saving my life, or at least my sanity. I recovered, later joined the military, and made a career out of it. When I was little, I used to play with my cars on my scars, since the one that runs up my arm looks like a road." He laughed. It turns out, Just Rick had been walking the trail for many years, one section at a time.

The trail community, the kindness of strangers, trail angels, trail magic, solitude, trees, open space—hikers say these are healing balms for the suffering. Maybe the rhythm of one's footsteps re-syncs the heart that has beat too fast for too long. Survival takes over on the AT—limping the next scramble, crossing fierce streams, searching for the next water source, finding shelter. Weather dominates; it's both a friend and enemy at times. For some, the arduous journey is the only retreat from the front line.

Wounded warriors say the trail humbles and heals them—it demands more than they have to give, but it also gives them more than they can take away. It teaches them how small they are against the infinite sky, the mountains, and the nights fractured by starlight, with no blood-stained field in sight.

WHAT'S NEXT?

Our life, exempt from public haunt, finds tongues in trees, books in the running brooks, sermons in stones, and good in everything.

William Shakespeare

EVERY YEAR, HUNDREDS OF MEN and women hike the trail as a way to navigate retirement. The AT, a feast of unkempt gardens and strange trees, draws them to review their lives. For some, it's a time to dust off old dreams that were never lived or imagine new ones. For others, during this exodus from their settled lives, it's a season for working through regrets. For all, it's a way to move, shed old skins and weight, and remember deep-down longings. Physical exertion becomes a friend, requiring more grit than maybe ever before. Many are out to prove to themselves and the world that they can do it.

Slim had long spider-like legs, a face reddened from the sun, with tiny scarlet capillaries traversing his cheeks and nose. Even from a few feet away, I could smell his breath. Scant gray-white hair made his baby blue eyes more striking. He was fifty-nine but looked older.

I met Slim when he was taking a zero-day on a gray morning in April. He sat on the couch, reading a book with a blanket tossed over his angular legs. He said this was his second time on the trail; the first was in 1987 when he was in his twenties.

"At that time, I was considered an old man on the trail. It was the young who ventured out. Today, there's a lot of us old guys out here, and like me, recently retired."

"A bit tougher now, I suspect," I said. "I know a lot of younger folks hit the trail looking for some revelation or transformation along the way."

"Who you are when you start the trail is the exact same person you are when you finish the trail," he said.

"I guess it's like traveling," I replied. "You go to a foreign country, and you realize you can't escape yourself or whatever is happening in your life; it lives in you. But it changed how I thought about the world, myself, and others; it expanded my mind and heart. Doesn't the trail do the same?"

"There are no new revelations on the trail," he said, returning to the book he was reading as if he had nothing more to say.

Aware of the young hiker sitting across from Slim, I attempted to engage him. He was wearing black jeans, a thick dark beard, a round face, frizzy bangs that hemmed his forehead; he looked to be in his mid-twenties. Most eye-catching, though, was the ten-inch knife sheathed at his side.

"I'm looking for work. Does the church need anything done?" he asked.

"Are you living on the trail?" I asked, trying to keep from staring at the knife.

"Working my way up and down it for the last eleven months."

"I can't think of anything we need to have done here. We're in pretty good shape; just had a cleanup day, when everyone pitches in." I waited a few seconds before asking him, "Are you hungry?"

"I've got three bags of rice; that'll get me through the next few days."

I offered him a few dollars to grab a couple of meals in town. The Village Farmer, just a short walk away, sold a hot dog and a piece of homemade pie for about two-fifty, a hiker's favorite, I told him. He hesitated at first, but then he reached out his hand and took the ten-dollar bill from mine and said thank you.

"Where are you headed after this?" I asked Killer, trying to let him know he was allowed only a two-night stay here.

"Not sure. Just somewhere in the woods. I'll find a town and see if I can get some work."

"Any plans to get off the trail at some point?"

"Not right now."

I wanted to question him, "Are you running away or toward something?" but didn't want to ask in front of Slim. I said goodbye, troubled inside for both the wandering young man and the older one who seemed just as homeless.

I met Early Riser later that week. He flashed his thick-soled marathon running shoes at me, said they had saved his knees over the Pennsylvania rocks, but now the shoes were destroyed, the soles too compressed and lopsided with wear. He was stocky, wore small framed black glasses, and his dark hair tousled as if he had just gotten out of the shower. He said he'd been on the trail for seventy days and had lost twenty pounds. He was in his early fifties. I asked how he had so much time to walk the trail.

"Just retired, sold my landscaping business, taking the time to hike the trail. I have a thirteen-year-old, a fifteen-year-old, and a nineteen-year-old." He shook his head, then said, "I miss them. They think it's great I'm out here doing this, but I don't know if I can stay away from them too much longer."

The years of physical labor showed in his thick hands, calloused palms, tree-trunk legs. His voice was gentle, with a lilt to it; I wondered where he called home. He smelled of wet earth, like the ground after a rain.

"What's next for you then, now that you sold your business?" I asked, standing near the door, as I could see he was getting ready to head into town for breakfast and to purchase a new pair of shoes.

"I don't know; that's why I'm out here, trying to figure that out. I know God's got something next for me. I just don't know what it is yet."

"You know, my brother recently retired. Before he left the hospital where he had worked for forty years, someone asked him, 'Is retirement going to be a bridge or a cliff?'"

"That's a great question. I have friends, many in law enforcement, who retired young, after twenty-five years of service, and died of one thing or other within a year."

"Maybe it has to do with a loss of identity, especially for those in high profile jobs," I added.

"I know, I know," he said. "It's scary."

I wondered if, having had a landscape business, he would spend even more time on the trail contemplating "the tongues in trees," as Shakespeare wrote. It had been an early spring with an explosion of flowers and bushes blooming too early and all at once. I wondered if he was itching, by habit alone, to be back home, rooting and uprooting things.

"So, you think you'll get off the trail, head home?"

"I miss my kids, my wife. Think I've hiked enough. I just want to go home."

Maybe that was the bridge, the revelation, that everything he had ever wanted, he had. Now, with the blessing of time, he could participate in his children's lives as he couldn't before.

"Will you do something different when you get home?" I asked.

"Still haven't figured it out. Maybe. I won't know until I stumble upon it."

How do we figure out what to do next in life? Does an epiphany come that one stumbles upon, as Early Riser had suggested? And if it happens this way, is it trustworthy, rather than if it slowly unfolds? I wanted to believe with him that every stage of our existence is both a genesis and a revelation.

STIRRINGS

But now, O Lord, You are our Father, We are the clay, and You our potter; And all of us are the work of Your hand.

Isaiah 64:8

WAYFARER PURCHASED AN MG MIDGET in Maine after completing the AT for his transportation home to Alabama, a green low-to-the-ground sports car that was forty years old. A few days before he would pass through Delaware Water Gap, he contacted me and asked if we could visit. It was late October 2018, a Saturday afternoon, when I met him at the church on a chilly day, but the sun was out, and the trees had finally started their turn toward winter.

When Wayfarer stepped out of his car, I remembered who he was; he had attended Sunday worship the morning after he bunked down here for a night and sat in the front row on a hot July day. There was some gravitational pull about him—maybe it was his prematurely thick, white, wavy hair or his eyes that were the color of glacial milk— soft and light green—with a depth that no one could guess. He was in his late thirties, which lent him the look of a man between worlds—not old, not young, or maybe both at the same time.

I asked him if he wanted to grab a boxed-lunch as part of a mission fundraiser a few blocks away when he arrived at the church. He agreed, and we piled into his car. I tried not to give voice to the groan in my bones as I lowered myself into the car that sat inches above the pavement.

At that moment and all the moments that followed, I wanted to forget that I was a pastor and decades older than him. We drove down the steep driveway and turned left onto Main Street. I felt like a twenty-year-old again, free of all the responsibilities I had had for most of my life, all the things I lugged, all the people I carried with me. Had it been slightly warmer, I would have requested that he fold the convertible top down. We would have to drive a much greater distance for that, I thought, amusing myself. The reality of my life, and vocation, and age stabbed my conscience and my joints. The MG Midget shimmied a bit in low gear as we climbed another steep road.

Liz, the woman who was cooking and serving the meal, greeted us, and after I bought lunch, she invited us to sit outside by the chiminea where a small wood fire burned, and the aromatic smoke penetrated the air. Wayfarer and I obliged. We opened our boxes and began to eat our hot chicken sandwiches as neighbors and other church folks came to join us.

Halfway through our lunch Liz came over to the table and explained that the fundraiser was to raise money to build a kiln for women in Kenya who created pottery to support their families. Liz had met the women on a recent mission trip; she had been learning the art of pottery since she retired from a government job in Washington, D.C., before marrying and moving to Delaware Water Gap.

What transpired next is difficult to explain. Wayfarer, we soon learned, is a well-known and accomplished potter. He showed us photographs of his work from his website—vessels that collapsed in on one another, melted into strange shapes, into beautiful deformities, into the unexpected.

"Tell me about your work. It's so unusual," I said.

"I've been working on perfecting a new technique that's never been done before. I use a flex material as I shape the clay, and when I fire it, the clay collapses, leans, falls, into itself or onto another vessel," he said. "What I learned from my work is how people perceived the work as a mistake, as flaws, as a deformity. The vessels are unpredictable on how they'll turn out, and people tend to miss the beauty in the brokenness. Instead, they focus on the expectation of what it was to be, rather than on its completeness, its wholeness, as it is."

"Seems to be a statement about the human condition and how we look at one another, doesn't it?" I said.

"When we size up a person, we always focus on what they lack, on their defects, on what is weak or imperfect, on their frailty, not on their strength or originality, or their entire being. But that's our stamp of humanity. Same's true for art."

I knew what he said was true; this way of seeing, of searching, and refusing to see the beauty in the things that fall inside us.

It turned out, Wayfarer had a lot of knowledge and experience in building kilns, having built a few himself. Liz explained how the women in Kenya fired their pottery by burying their clay pots inside a grass-fed fire. She hoped to have a kiln built for them from the region's natural elements.

"The bricks would have to be brought in," Wayfarer said as if he knew of the ground upon which these women lived and worked. "And there are few trees so that it couldn't be a wood-burning kiln. You'd have to build a propane kiln."

Liz brought out her tablet and showed Wayfarer photos she had taken of the Kenyan women at work, of the blackened grasses, the unglazed vessels; vessels that sang of genesis and Africa, its wildness, its exotic beauty. The pots were unglazed and porous, made from thick, hardened red earth that was etched and painted with geometric designs. Designs that I thought reflected the way the African sun beats down, how the rivers wend through shale, the way the wind blows throughout the savannas, and the way the acacia trees bend.

After, Liz invited us to see her pottery creations in her art studio upstairs in the barn-like garage. Wayfarer lifted and cupped each piece in his hand, ran his fingers over the glaze, turned each one over, and inspected the base. Another bowl reflected Kenya with an acacia tree and a raised tangle of a river with the blue sky inside. Watching him hold each of the many pieces on display, it seemed he was listening to each work of art with his hands and eyes, as if the clay spoke, and he felt the dark fire in each vessel.

What happened is even harder to explain—the confluence of having Wayfarer visit on this day, the only day of the fundraiser, at that time of day, with his deep experience in this art, and guiding Liz on what kiln would work and what wouldn't work, simply was undeniably God-ordained.

It seemed so, at least to Liz and to me, who would end up talking about the timing of his visit in the days to come. Moreover, we were convinced that Wayfarer would end up going to Kenya to help build a kiln one day in the future.

WHAT WE CARRY

Returning home is the most difficult part of long-distance hiking; You have grown outside the puzzle and your piece no longer fits.

Cindy Ross

WAYFARER AND I DROVE BACK to the church. I expected he would soon be on his way since he wanted to make it to Virginia before dark, where he would stay with friends he had made on the AT. Yet, we sat and talked for a long while about his hiking experience. It was rare to speak to a hiker after completing the trail as most traveled home by the quickest route. We settled into two white plastic chairs outside Fellowship House with the sun at our backs. Wayfarer began to speak about post-trail depression.

"A lot of hikers will tell you that hiking the trail ruined their lives," he said. "Every day, hikers wake up with a goal—to make it to Mount Katahdin, to the finish line, and when they get there, they realize that there's nothing there but rocks and holes."

As he spoke, I envisioned him on that final step up the mountain, exhaustion in his bones, tightness in his muscles, sweat on his brow, and the emotional surrender. I felt the long pause before imagining him climbing back down through the wilderness, feeling more homeless than ever.

He continued, "They had a goal of how many miles to hike every day. They had a purpose and found meaning in it. They were moving every day, meeting new people, sleeping in different places every night. They truly believe that when they make that final ascent up

Katahdin that they'll have all of this conclusion, all things answered, that they'll find the ultimate purpose of their life. But when you get there, you say to yourself, okay, where do I go from here? What am I going to do now? You say to yourself, okay, hiking the trail gave me a purpose, but at the top, what is the meaning of it all? And rather than answering that, they keep on going; they hike other trails. It becomes an addiction. They have a difficult time going back to the lives they lived before hiking the trail."

I asked, "So are they trying to convince themselves that with the next hike, they will reach whatever conclusion they thought they would reach on Katahdin?"

"I think so," he said.

Wayfarer hadn't lived a conventional life, but I could sense in him a reluctance to return to life as it had been. After all, he had left that life for a season on the trail due to some restlessness, some holy or unholy discontentment.

"At the top of Katahdin, there are no blazes to tell you where to go now, where to stay, or who to meet," he said.

As he spoke, I recalled the story of his family, now when he was barely a teen, his father gave away their house and car, piled his wife and five children into a conversion van, and traveled east, according to what he believed God called him to do. In a sense, I thought Wayfarer had done the same thing, only he went solo and gave away everything to go on his exodus last spring. An exodus into a lush wilderness of mountains and trees and meadows and fields.

"The trail is just a trial. Life is full of them—you don't have to go twenty-two hundred miles looking for one. So many people focus on the trail, and then they think they'll find meaning, but there's always another one and then another one. You get to the end, and you realize there's nothing there; yes, you had a great experience, but it doesn't have meaning in itself. It solves nothing. So they look forward, they go on another hike, hike another trail—get their triple crown—walk the Pacific Crest Trail, the AT, and the Continental Divide Trail," he continued. "They love the process, but they keep walking in a circle. I should know. I went to the trail looking for fulfillment, for what's next—that's what drew me, those deep-seated questions. I wanted to find meaning in it. I learned that meaning could only derive from Christ; everything outside of Christ goes to waste—ultimately, it's Christ that brings meaning to life. I learned what Christ taught—that the quintessential element of life is love—to love God and love one another—if we can just work on that in any trial that we're in, which usually involves other people. People don't know where to look."

Maybe there is nothing heavier in all the world than emptiness, and people carry it wherever they go, I wanted to say.

An hour had passed. He said he had to go as it was getting late, and we hugged goodbye. As we did, I thought about all the hikers that had come and gone from the hostel over the last five years since I had been a part of this ministry, about all the men and women my arms had held, knowing it was likely that I wouldn't see them again. I wondered if they suffered post-trail depression, as Wayfarer had said. It was true; many who hiked the trail would come back in the years to come, hiking it once again.

I remember them. I still carry them with me and will, as long as I live.

RATTLESNAKE SWAMP TRAIL

Nothing in all creation is so like God as stillness.

Meister Eckhart

S OUNDS MOVED SLUGGISHLY IN THE muggy air the last days of July 2017 as if every living thing was slowly drowning. The dense air thickened the organic fragrance of pine and pond, of fallen trees and rotting wood. Fish didn't dare jump until late at night when the quarter moon shone—though the temperature barely dipped. Impervious, the mosquitos whined and fed on us victims without mercy.

During this unbearable heat, six of us from church had met at the Mohican Outdoor Center to embark on a three-day spiritual retreat on the AT under the leadership of David Childs, half-man, half-wilderness. The purpose of this short foray into the woods was to build community, to learn to live by land rather than by technology, and, I figured out before too long, to push us harder than we'd ever push ourselves.

Everything within me—the inexperienced hiker—ached beyond decibels that first night after we had humped water, gear, food, and equipment to our site on the edge of Catfish Pond near Blairstown, New Jersey, about twelve miles from Delaware Water Gap. After we set up camp, we hiked one portion of Rattlesnake Swamp Trail in the afternoon, a several-mile segment of the AT, a steep, rocky stairway to heaven that felt like hell to climb. My veins, like swollen rivers, felt as if they were about to burst their banks. That night, the ground beneath my spine was stone hard, despite the thin comfort pad under my sleeping bag.

Waves of claustrophobia suffocated me as the nylon ceiling of my tent hung only inches over my head. The night air, miserable with heat, pressed inside my lungs that felt as if they were collapsing. I couldn't unzip my tent fast enough to free myself from this thin-walled prison to breathe, and when I did emerge and announced that I was having a panic attack and a hot flash all at once, nobody came to my rescue. They either laughed or snored through my heat-anxiety wave.

"I'm preaching about compassion this Sunday, and I'm going to use every one of you as a sermon illustration," I said. I wasn't sure what I was looking for—maybe not to feel so alone. I forced myself to crawl back into the tent, rocks pressing into my knees, breathing as slowly and deeply as I could.

Before six the following morning, unsure whether I had slept for more than a few minutes and keenly aware of every bone in my skeletal structure, I moved carefully so that the bones snapped back into their sockets. Liz, one of my fellow hikers, had unzipped her tent and stepped out. I soon followed, wiggling my way out of my cocoon that faced the southern edge of the pond, and limped toward the boulders perched like thrones above the small lake. Liz and I exchanged a few words, but we were both drawn into the silence. White mist moved over the surface of the water like angels bathing before anyone saw them, playing on treetops on the ridge opposite the lake, baptizing us with dew. The scent of honeysuckle laced every breath. The soundscape around us—birds chirping, insects buzzing, branches rustling with wildlife, the stir of water—were more life-affirming than any sermon.

David had quoted Thoreau as we sat in a circle the night before and shared why we had come on the trip. Every one of us was over fifty, except Gary, who was in his early thirties. David knew the quote by heart, and he recited it:

> *I went to the woods because I wished to live deliberately,*
> *to front only the essential facts of life, and see if I could*
> *not learn what it had to teach, and not, when I came to*

die, discover that I had not lived. I did not wish to live what was not life, living is so dear; nor did I wish to practice resignation, unless it was quite necessary.

I wanted to live deep and suck out all the marrow of life, to live so sturdily and Spartan-like as to put to rout all that was not life, to cut a broad swath and shave close, to drive life into a corner, and reduce it to its lowest terms . . .

I contemplated the words "to live deep" as I sat on a boulder. Had I lived deep? Was I living deeply enough? Ministry had required everything inside of me and always more, resulting in constant wrestling with God, whom I had finally learned, always wins, but who wants to be contended with, who wants to be held on to; to turn, face him and fight with him, if need be, rather than with others. Because of this, God has left me injured in the place only He could wound; that was for certain. But I, too, had injured God.

Years earlier, I had lived too deep in misery. I wandered in a dark wood; it didn't feel like morning for a long time. I finally understood that to live deep means I have to be willing to allow the most painful things in my life to do their excavation. I've discovered that my spirit, what some call the soul, has endless depth. I learned not to be so afraid to be lost or to wander or to walk with a limp.

I thought of these things as I studied the immovable sky, the mountainous ridge, the water—the trinity of the throbbing natural world.

Glancing over at Liz, I wondered about the things that swam in her blood. I knew a little about her history, growing up in the South with her grandmother, a black woman barber born on the islands. Liz taught me every day about the discrepancies between our worlds and the trials of her climb to success as an African-American woman in a government job. She was a lady, always dressed to the meticulous hilt. This was her first foray into the wilderness, sleeping in a tent and hiking. Still, she maintained her fashion sense, her manicured beauty, and her lovely dignity, unlike me.

By six-thirty, the rest of the crew had awakened, a few men heading into the woods to relieve themselves; all were rubbing sleep from their eyes (that I envied since I had none in my own) and finger-combing their hair. The privy, located a bit of a distance from camp, was strung with cobwebs inside. Sunlight seeped through the seams of the wooden enclosure, but it was still so dark inside you couldn't see yourself or the spiders that crawled everywhere. I shivered against the imagined sensation of their legs on mine. The toilet sat over what appeared to be a bottomless pit. In the heat, I expected the privy to be stinkier than it was. It was easy to understand why only one in four hikers completes the trail and why most quit within the first two hundred miles.

I left the boulder of my contemplation and walked toward David with an exaggerated hitch in my giddyup. Then asked, "So, David, what exactly is the relationship between suffering and spirituality?"

True to David, he just laughed and continued his preparations for breakfast, heating water over a small propane burner for oatmeal, instant coffee, and hot cocoa. I knew the answer to that, as did he. Suffering has beauty buried deep within it. It shatters walls and barriers that separate us from one another; it teaches us who we are; reveals our vulnerabilities. In other words, it smacks its lips of truths few ever want to hear.

I joined the others in retrieving food from the bear box at the outer edge of the campsite. Cooking over a propane burner lacked the joy of a campfire, and I missed the aroma of burning wood and its fragrant smoke that would carry me instantly back to places I always wanted to be. We gathered around the picnic table, and it was as if our stomachs were hollow; we gorged on multiple servings of instant oatmeal, fresh oranges, nuts, and hunks of cheese.

After breakfast, we filled our daypacks with trail mix, water bottles, lunch, flashlights, rain gear, and cell phones, then grabbed our hiking poles and headed back to the trail. It was about nine-thirty then. I couldn't help but ask, "Really? Flashlights? We're going to be out that long?"

To which David responded, "You never know. Got to be prepared," and then he let out a sadistic chuckle.

At the base of Rattlesnake Swamp Trail, David lectured us about timber rattlesnakes and how they hide in the cleft of logs and stones.

"Be mindful not to step on one" was the essence of his instruction.

The trail was named after the large rattlesnake den located across the lake in the rocky hillside, not far from where we stood.

"Rattlesnakes can swim on the surface," he informed us. "You'll see their heads and their rattle above water. Every fall, when cold weather sets in, the snakes return to where they were born. We're going to turn left and head up the trail in a different direction. Who's going to lead?"

Liz, peering up at the Rattlesnake Swamp Trail sign, said, "You know, in all the horror movies, it's always the black person who gets killed first."

We laughed. Our laughter was one considerable part anxiety, I was sure, for our ignorance of what it means to be black in America and how blacks are often portrayed or killed off in Hollywood movies. She decided not to lead or to be the sweep, the one who stays at the back of the line.

The slow and steady ascent on the narrow, uneven, sharp stone path began through a dense forest of mountain laurel, hemlock, and rhododendron. We walked through sticky webs along the way, then checked ourselves for spiders. We listened for wild animals and watched for bears, a common sight here, as we trekked for what seemed like forever before stopping for a water break and freeing ourselves from the weight of our daypacks.

This was work. This demanded more determination than I had in me. I wondered out loud how anyone could walk the trail day after day, week after week, month after month, remembering how many a hiker told me it becomes a job, a game of survival, life boiled down to food, water, and shelter. We passed a few thru-hikers on the way who were resting, lighting up hand-rolled cigarettes whose smoke stained the air.

David showed us how to collect water from its earthen source at the hollow place between the roots of a tree where water dripped down into a slim brook. The water flowed cold and bright, and we filled our bottles after eating our peanut butter and jam sandwiches and munching on trail mix. Up steep inclines, we continued, the blistering heat threatening to defeat me time and time again, but what choice did I have but to continue? I had to stop often to catch my breath, to wipe my brow, to gulp water.

Several hours into our hike, we came to the ridge overlooking farmlands, fields, and rivers. Half the group had climbed up Catfish Fire Tower, several stories high, when they spotted a thunderstorm off to the west, moving toward us.

"We've got to get off the ridge before it hits," David said with enough alarm in his voice that we picked up our pace for the downward trek. Going downhill was more difficult than going uphill, though gravity was not a friend in either direction. Our knees stretched out of their caps. We could feel the dagger rocks through the soles of our shoes as we dug the points of our hiking poles into the dusty seams of the ground.

We didn't converse much with each other until closing the distance between ourselves and the campsite. En route, we passed a group of young adult volunteers performing trail maintenance, digging up "human-sized stones," moving them to level out the pathway, and removing fallen trees. A few pelts of rain marked our sweat-drenched clothes, but the storm passed over us. At the base of the trail, we collapsed on a bench outside a vacant cabin. A few of us, I included, groaned and moaned in unison as we unloaded our packs. Each one of us, slathered with slimy sweat, hobbled like all the hikers that come to the center. Nerves in our feet had gone numb from the weight we'd carried too far and too long. We returned to camp seven hours after we had left, around four-thirty that afternoon.

After breakfast the following morning, we prepared to separate from the group to "solo." I took my journal and returned to the now-familiar boulder. The pleasurable taste of the coffee percolated on my tongue and in the atmosphere around the campsite. Sun warmed my muscles and eased their aches but choked my lungs as there was not even a stir of breeze. Human clatter waned as we each made our way to a private designated place for a time of solitude and reflection. In the words of Thoreau, we went into the woods to "suck the marrow" out of the experience. For me, the experience had sucked the marrow out of my bones! I knew there was a wilderness inside me, a wild place forgotten in the rush of my life. I knew it was essential for me to draw a map to navigate my way back to this forgotten place inside me that howled in the night, whimpered in the morning, and echoed during the day.

I sketched the campsite in my journal. I wrote about the morning bird song, the rustling of fellow campers, the sound of my pen scratching on paper as I attempted to unearth the beauty that was beneath all the aches and pains of the strenuous hikes, the frayed muscles, the sleepless nights, the draining heat. The six of us had leaned on each other, and upon God, I was sure, as we strained forward. In some strange way, I could feel where their weight had pressed against me even though I was alone.

As I wrote, I realized it was August 2nd, the day that would have been my forty-second wedding anniversary, had the marriage not ended after seventeen years. A sapling quivered but I felt no wind.

I sat, staring out into the sky and woods, inviting those same winds to blow the seeds of wildness into the fertile field of me, the same ground where children grew, where words were nurtured, where God lived. Upon that rock, in the stillness, I felt those seeds in my hands and on my skin. They passed through my eyes into that invisible garden within me.

A few hours later, around noon, we climbed down a ladder of boulders to gather in a circle on a small grassy spot at the edge of the lake. We shared what each one of us wanted to leave behind on this retreat and what each one of us wanted to take away. Then we lit a candle, broke a loaf of bread, passed it around, dipping a hunk of it into a cup of grape juice, partaking of it one at a time. I tasted the sun, the trees, and humanity in that cup as the juice-soaked bread slipped down my throat like a benediction of light.

More storms were coming. A few of us were suffering knee and foot injuries that made hiking less of an option, so we dismantled the campsite and humped everything back to our vehicles, and headed into town for lunch before returning home. Gary called his wife while we waited for omelets, toast, and burgers, only to learn that she had been in a car accident, having fallen asleep at the wheel on her commute home the day before, sideswiping an 18-wheeler. She had been up all night with their sick toddler. She wasn't injured, although the car was damaged.

The world was quick to intrude; the wilderness we had found within us burrowed deeper, out of sight, as I had imagined it did for every section and thru-hiker who re-enters the reality of family, responsibilities, and current affairs. But the deeper the wilderness burrowed within me, I knew the greater, and more profound, a life I could live.

BENEDICTION

You venture out into the wilds where you have to depend on your intuition, on Nature's way, on your deeper sense of belonging. What some call faith or spirituality is that risking, that longing and belonging.

Chris Highland

W INTER IS A BENEDICTION TO the hiking season, even though a few hearty SOBO hikers trail into the center in December. There is something about the shudder of cold, snow's silent fall, and avoiding stressful holidays in the darkest months that the few venture out into the exquisite beauty of winter. There is a complete sense of loneliness then—yet a feeling as if one is never alone.

Tinsel-like icicles sparkle rainbows over white fields as the sun beams down on them, a promise that all storms will pass. Ice-coated branches clink against each other when the air riffles through them, sounding like wind chimes or small hands clapping. Frozen lakes and ponds emit high-pitched groans and moans, like shrill screams that ricochet from shore to shore beneath the ice. Winter air, scrubbed clean and pure.

Throughout my tenure here, hikers confess that fields and forests grow in their bloodstreams now, and the wilderness calls out day and night, beckoning them to listen to all it has to say. Nature awakened them to the hidden choir that resides in everything—the music of rocks and roots, the chorus of rain and river, the blues of storm and silence—in all that is.

What they fear when they return to their lives is that they will forget to inhale grace with every breath and fail to experience the resurrection that comes every morning when dawn seeps into their lungs and wiggles beneath their skin to rouse them. But I know, the seeds of longing for a more profound and authentic life never die when buried so deep.

ACKNOWLEDGMENTS

I want to thank the people of The Presbyterian Church of the Mountain for all they have taught and shown me about genuine hospitality. They provide care for the wounded, shelter and water for the thirsty, and food to nourish the body and soul. I could not have asked for a more beautiful faith community to shepherd, ever.

I want to acknowledge and thank my daughters, Erin and Lindsay, my son, and my grandchildren, Dakotah, Harley, and Destiny, for your presence, love, and encouragement. Additionally, I owe a debt of gratitude to my mother, Shirley, my sister, Sandy, and my brothers Craig and Jeffrey Blackman. Their belief in me has never faltered. Thank you for walking alongside me on this trail called life. Lastly, I would be remiss not also to acknowledge my long-time faithful friend, Cynthia Carlaw, whose creativity stuns me every day. Thank you, thank you, thank you.

ABOUT THE AUTHOR:

Sherry Blackman is the pastor of The Presbyterian Church of the Mountain in Delaware Water Gap, Pennsylvania, home to the oldest, continuously-running Hiker Hostel on the Appalachian Trail. She is an award-winning journalist, poet, and author of *Call to Witness: A True Story of one woman's battle with a disability, discrimination, and a pharmaceutical powerhouse*, published in 2013. In addition, Rev. Blackman is a chaplain for the Pennsylvania State Police. Her forth-coming book, *Rev-It-Up: Tales of a Truck Stop Chaplain*, due out in 2022, chronicles her adventures as a Truck Stop Chaplain, a ministry she's served since 2006.

CPSIA information can be obtained
at www.ICGtesting.com
Printed in the USA
BVHW062347010322
630323BV00001B/49